Accession no.
36161

D0268734

Sharing Possessions

Sharing Possessions

What Faith Demands

• •

SECOND EDITION

Luke Timothy Johnson

LIS - LIBRARY

Date	Fund
2/5/12.	r-che.

Order No.
2297942 -

University of Chester

WILLIAM B. EERDMANS PUBLISHING COMPANY

GRAND RAPIDS, MICHIGAN / CAMBRIDGE, U.K.

© 2011 Luke Timothy Johnson

All rights reserved

Published 2011 by

Wm. B. Eerdmans Publishing Co.

2140 Oak Industrial Drive N.E., Grand Rapids, Michigan 49505 /

P.O. Box 163, Cambridge CB3 9PU U.K.

Printed in the United States of America

17 16 15 14 13 12 11   7 6 5 4 3 2 1

ISBN 978-0-8028-0399-3

www.eerdmans.com

Contents

Preface to the Second Edition

Almost thirty years have passed since *Sharing Possessions* first appeared in 1981. This second edition provides the opportunity to reflect on the circumstances of its composition, its character, and the author's present appreciation of a work undertaken in (relative) youth rather than (creeping) senescence.

The book arose out of two specific and personal factors. The first was my recent completion of a dissertation, *The Literary Function of Possessions in Luke-Acts* (Yale, 1976). In that study I grappled with the fact that although Luke consistently speaks about possessions he does not speak about possessions consistently. I saw that to come to grips with possessions in that biblical writing required approaching it at a level other than ethical admonition — I saw that Luke used language about possessions symbolically, as a way of expressing human responses to God and other persons.

More important, when I wrote this book, I was in a period of difficult personal adjustment with respect to possessions. I had been a Benedictine monk living within a community of possessions. But now I was married with seven children (six of them inherited), and responsible for acquiring and disposing of possessions in a manner I had never anticipated while living as a monk. I was learning that the meaning of "being" and "having" was much more complicated than I had earlier thought. Chapter 2, I vividly recall, was written over a weekend sequestered in a New Haven motel, temporarily removed from the demands of parenthood. With respect to the connection between faith and the faithful use of possessions, I found, Scripture was inconsistent and life was deeply ambiguous.

My effort to think through these things appeared in a Fortress Press series called "Overtures to Biblical Theology," and the placement in this series helped shape my project. My book takes the entire Bible seriously, and it tries to provide an example of theological thinking on the basis of the Bible that at once engages the realities of concrete human existence and the complexities of the scriptural texts. I stated in the original preface, "I remain fuzzy on many issues, but I am sure of this — scholarship is not the same thing as theology." That distinction still makes sense to me. I consider theology as a form of personal witness more than as an assemblage of opinions.

The approach to theological thinking in this early book is one that I have followed in subsequent works.

1. I am convinced that theology, as an inductive art, must begin with careful attention to real life. Before we can engage Scripture on any question, we need to have a better notion of what the question really is. Here, I begin with the slipperiness of everyday language about possessions, and move from there to the still more ambiguous subject of the embodied human existence, the mystery that lies at the heart of being and having.

2. In turning to Scripture, it is essential to determine the limits of its witness. In this case, I show that the search for a clear and unequivocal mandate with respect to possessions is stymied by the complexity found in even a single witness, Luke-Acts.

3. I take the fundamental theological topic to be the drama enacted by God and humans that is marked, from the side of humans, by the opposed responses of idolatry and faith. The use of possessions is *theologically* significant, I argue, as it symbolizes (or expresses) human responses to the living God and God's creation.

4. Having made that fundamental theological connection, it is possible to consider the diverse ways in which the respective biblical witnesses speak of possessions as the "symbol" as well as the "mandate" of faith.

5. Finally, in light of this theological perspective, it is also possible to critically evaluate actual Christian practices with respect to the use of possessions.

The approach, even after thirty years, still seems right to me. For this new edition, therefore, I have kept the basic text of the original book intact. I do not mean thereby to suggest that it is without flaws, only that any effort to correct those flaws might introduce other and more serious deficiencies.

Instead of editing the original text, I have added several paragraphs of comment at the end of each section. These comments expand on or modify elements in the original text in light of my subsequent thinking. In addition, I have added a substantial epilogue, which takes into account further work that I have done on the subject, some of the contributions made by other writers of which I am aware, and those things that some readers have thought to be in need of correction *(corrigenda)*, as well as some things that, after a long time thinking on the matter, I considered important to add *(addenda)*.

To have a book find its way back into print after a considerable time in hibernation is deeply gratifying to the author. I hope that it proves useful to those readers who read it now for the first time. I must thank the initiative and encouragement of Michael Thomson and the patient support of the staff at Eerdmans. Thanks also to those students and congregations who have generously continued to receive these ideas. Thanks above all to the persons mentioned in the original dedication who have gifted my life.

LUKE TIMOTHY JOHNSON
October 10, 2009

Introduction

This book is written as an exercise in theological reflection on one of the knottiest questions imaginable: the connection between being a Christian and the way we own and use things. The book is intended to provoke thought. Thinking, to be sure, is hard work. Thinking about our lives is even harder. Thinking about our lives as Christians with any degree of specificity is worse yet. And when we turn to thinking about money and possessions, we find ourselves in murky waters. The things we own and use, like our sexuality, lie close to the bone of our individual and collective sense of identity. It's hard for us to step back and reflect dispassionately about matters in which our passions are, by definition, very much involved.

I will not try to present you with a neatly wrapped package of biblical teaching about possessions and the use of possessions. One reason for this is that I am not sure there is such a package. Another reason is that, even if there were and we could appropriate it, such a package might be just one more possession of whose significance we have not a notion. A good part of the thinking in this book, however, will be devoted to the question of how the Bible speaks to this mystery of human possessing and possessiveness.

A good place to begin thinking about possessions and the use of possessions is at puzzlement. What a strange and ambiguous sort of topic this is! No sooner do we begin thinking than we must pull up short and examine the tools of our thinking: our images and words. The words we employ are of common stock: "to own," "to have," "rich," "poor," "equality." Because they are commonly employed words, they are filled with the ambiguity of everyday language. We say "She has a good mind," "He has a well-

1

conditioned body," or "They have a lovely house." Does the verb "to have" carry the same meaning in each of these sentences? Does a person "have" a body or mind in the same way that one "has" a house or farm? Clearly not. For one thing, a house or farm is firmly fixed outside a person, whereas the mind and body are integral to being a person, somehow "in here" rather than "out there." Our language, in fact, supposes a hierarchy of interiority, in which the mind is more "in here" than the body. We more easily say "my body" than "the body's me." The ambiguity of physical existence in the world lies at the heart of the mystery of possessions, and we must return to this puzzle. Another difference between having a house and having a body is the degree of disposability in each case. You and I can exchange houses more easily than bodies. The heartfelt cry, "I wish I could get inside your head!" is denied realization to all save neurosurgeons. But we get inside each other's houses with ease and enjoy walking across fields owned by others. I can also give my house away without essential loss to myself. If I try to separate myself from my body (see how intricate the language is in this possession talk?), I run the real risk of putting an end to being, altogether. Where I go, my body goes; my house doesn't. In fact, there is always a certain fictive quality to ownership of things outside the body. Fields and farms, stocks and deposit boxes, are subject to challenge and seizure. We must tend them, guard them, secure them by legal writ or force of arms. Generally, I can safely claim to own something when I can effectively assert my power over it. The relationship between power and possessions is another part of the puzzle to which we should return.

Now, the ambiguity of our language about owning and having is manifest when I realize that all the distinctions I have been making can be questioned or denied. It has happened with disturbing frequency that the difference between "having a body" and "having a house" has been demolished. People's bodies have become the property of others, and even the means of commercial exchange. People's minds have been "possessed" by others. Slavery and mind-control are usually facilitated by a simple adjustment in perspective, which in itself testifies to the distinctions I have been making and which alone renders claims of ownership over human beings plausible. The adjustment consists of refusing to recognize as human the one claimed as property; humans are defined as chattel or subjects. It is a brilliant stratagem, breathtaking in its simplicity and efficiency. At the very least, the possibility of possessions language being employed in this fashion should alert us to the shifty character of our topic.

There is no less confusion in our talk about rich and poor. We sometimes use these terms as though they were univocal, but of course they are not. They are, first of all, correlative. When I say "rich," I at least imply a comparison, "rich compared with this or that." Where there is no concept of "poor," there can be little meaning in the term "rich." The statement, "America is rich in resources," is vague not only about the sort of resources meant but also about the scale of reference implied. America's resources are rich compared with whose? Africa's? Malaysia's? Australia's? The sentence, "I live in a poor neighborhood," involves a comparison with other neighborhoods that can be called rich, or at least an understood scale of measurement into which various neighborhoods can be placed.

Not only are the two terms correlative, they are also, each of them, relative. There are degrees of rich and poor: "rich, richer, richest"; "wealthy, affluent, opulent"; "poor, poorer, poorest"; and "deprived, needy, destitute." All of these, in turn, are related to the standards of diverse cultures. It takes much less to be rich in Ghana than in Manhattan; a beggar of Calcutta would not automatically recognize a denizen of the South Bronx as a fellow "poor person."

It is difficult as well to distinguish quantitative and qualitative aspects of these words. A glance back at the statements I just used as examples shows this clearly. In what *sense* is America or my neighborhood rich, or poor? Even when we try to use the words "rich" and "poor" in a strictly denotative way, within the range of economic factors, the terms tend to contain other qualitative, value-laden connotations. To be rich tends also to mean "to be powerful" and, frequently, "to be happy," and, often enough, "to be happy at someone else's expense." In the same way, the phrase "to be poor" tends to mean "to be powerless," and, frequently, "to be unhappy," and, often enough, "to be miserable because of the oppressive actions of the rich." These qualitative aspects creep into our language even when we are consciously aware that there are some people who are voluntarily poor but seem to be happy, people who are involuntarily poor who claim to be content, and people who have lots of money and power who commit suicide.

The terms "rich" and "poor" stand as symbols for other things. Sometimes the symbols become stereotypes and sometimes the instruments of propaganda or demagoguery. Even when they do not, however, they carry for all of us whole constellations of significance and emotional resonance. In the United States today, in spite of a standard of living which is an object of both wonder and scandal to much of the rest of the world, one would find surprisingly few people willing to admit, "Yes, I am really wealthy." Certain claims and burdens seem to be attached to such an acknowledgment; there is an embarrassment connected with the bald confession of wealth. It is easier for some to say, "I am not really that well off." On the other hand, we might find equally few people ready to admit without equivocation, "Yes, I am genuinely poor," for that admission, too, carries with it other meanings. Many would feel more comfortable saying, "I am not, after all, that bad off."

These disclaimers of wealth or poverty assume a scale of measurement. The scale itself is flexible, depending on society's perception of itself and comparison with other societies. The "level of poverty" fixed by the bureaucracy for welfare payments in the United States is a figure many times higher than the level of relative affluence in some other lands. The sliding scale upon which rich and poor perch precariously is also symbolically ambiguous. The measure of "economic worth" (meaning, one supposes, the money one would get for the sale of all one has) can easily become, and is frequently employed, as a measure of "personal worth." The reluctance to admit great wealth may be an avoidance of hubris, and the denial of destitution may be a claim to human worth, given the connotations of placement on this symbolic scale.

Another term that is frequently used in discussions about possessions, especially when the focus is social, is a term that, if anything, is even more confusing than the others I have been discussing. It has been a part of the slogan of political revolution — "Liberty, Equality, Fraternity." It has been a principle of constitutional law — "All men are created equal." It is a bone of legislative and litigative contention — "equal rights," "equal opportunity." It is a Utopian dream — "all share equally." For ancient Greek philosophers, it was an ideal of community life — "friendship is equality." But what is meant by equality when the term is used of possessions? Cutting an apple pie into eight demonstrably equal slices is fairly easy. After that, the equal distribution of goods gets hopelessly and endlessly entangled in qualitative considerations. The problems of distributive justice have exercised the minds of philosophers since Aristotle. An apparently straightforward measurement of things and their relative worth can become, in a wink, the measurement of persons and their worth. Sometimes Utopian thinkers have considered that by making all possessions "equal" they have made all persons "equal," and that by eliminating possessions as a possible measure of worth, they have eliminated the problem of possessiveness. They have not; they have only moved it to another realm. And far from eliminating possessions as a measure, they have used them vigorously in just that way.

These preliminary musings about the language we use in talking about possessions are intended as a reminder that this is a slippery subject with which we find ourselves involved. We should not be overly confident that we have the slightest idea of what we are talking about. The difficulty, of course, lies not only in the language, but in the reality toward which the language points.

Part of the problem with possessions is that we persist in thinking about them as a problem. They are not, and even my talking about the pieces of a puzzle distorts the reality. When we think about possessions and the use of possessions, we are not thinking about geometric theorems. We are thinking about a fundamental aspect of human existence, about the disposition of human freedom. A problem, as Gabriel Marcel has reminded us, lies "out there," like a crossword puzzle. However tangled, a problem, with sufficient effort and intelligence, can be "reduced," "solved," "eliminated." It is "objective" and at least potentially resolvable. But when we think about human ownership, we are thinking about a mystery. A mystery has to do with the dimensions of human existence in the world, with "being" in the world, with our own lives involved in and called to by Being. We cannot be objective about this sort of mystery. We cannot be detached from our own lives the way we can and should be about the fixing of the carburetor of our cars. We cannot pull ourselves away from our own existence and look at it as though it were a crossword puzzle; that way lies alienation.

Thinking about possessions, therefore, demands, first of all, not the approach of problem solving but the approach of reflection, or meditation, through which the human spirit leans back and contemplates its own activity. To begin to approach the mystery of human owning and possessing, we need to ponder the phenomenon itself. When we speak of owning things, what do we mean? What sort of claim are we making about ourselves and the world about us? What is involved in saying "this is mine" and "that is yours"? How do we get from "in here" to "out there"? Because human existence in this world is irreducibly somatic, we need to ponder in particular the relationship between the human body and possessions. In what sense "have I" a body and in what sense "am I" a body? If possessions and the use of possessions are an extension of myself, where is the line drawn between the "self" and the "thing"? We cannot think seriously about possessions unless we are willing to enter this messy place where human freedom and the disposition of the body impinge on each other.

To think seriously about possessions one needs to recognize, too, that our language about and perceptions of possessions are located within a societal and symbolic context. We stand within a given society's appreciation of what it means to have and own, and we can compare these valuations with those of other societies. But these valuations are themselves located within overarching and pervasive understandings about what being human means for a given culture. Thinking and talking about possessions, in other words, assumes not only a sociology but an anthropology and theology as well. To use less rarified terms, the ways people regard owning things and the values they attach to possessions involve the ways they think about human nature (or human freedom in the world), about the place of humans within the world, and about the relationship of human beings and the world to God.

We are scarcely the first people to give hard thought to such matters. Most of the basic views of possessions, and ideas of how they should be used, were in place before the time of Jesus. Much of the thinking and programming of recent generations on these questions has been a commentary on those ancient options. In fact, the ancient writings stand as particularly valuable stimulants to our own reflection. Our task here, after all, is to think about a fundamental aspect of human existence. The complexities of contemporary cultures, the implications of technology, and the peculiar dynamics of global economic interdependence make the situation appear impossible and forbidding. But the issues still come down to the claims being made by human beings about themselves and the things they say they own. Since the writings of antiquity were addressed to situations of considerably less economic complexity, but in which the impulses of the human spirit are all too recognizable, the fundamental issues are the more easily identified in them.

In the last chapter of this book, I will look in some detail at two of these ancient models for the use of possessions and inquire into the perceptions concerning God and the world that appear to underlie them. I will try to determine how consonant these ideals are with the perception of Christianity regarding possessions. But before that can be done, the obvious questions must be these: Is there such a Christian perception, and, if there is, where can it be found? Unless we have a standpoint from which to discern these options, these plans for the use of possessions, we will flounder. Our first task, then, is to locate and reflect upon the Christian ideal regarding possessions, or at least to ask whether there is such an ideal. What source can we turn to for this? Our instinctive response would be the Bible. And this instinctive response is the correct one. If reflection on our Christian existence is to be theological in the proper sense, then that reflection must actively engage the normative texts of Christian identity, the Old and New Testaments.

For Christian theology, the Bible does not stand as just one more example of an ancient writing of antiquarian interest but as the unnormed norm of our ecclesial and individual lives of faith. To provide this sort of fundamental impetus to our reflection, however, the Bible must be appropriated in something other than a purely historical fashion. The method of history can answer only historical questions, not axiological ones. The historian, including the "biblical theologian," can describe the place of these ancient writings within the historical development of Judaism or early Christianity and convey the "message" of the writings to those historical periods. But for the Bible to be appropriated as the enduring norm of the church's life in every age, another perspective must be adopted — one that is given not by science, but by faith. That is, the Bible must be listened to not only as the words of human writers, but as the Word of God to every age of the church. When the church (and the theologian who reflects within the seeking faith of the church) reads its canon of sacred writings *as* canon, that is, as prophetic, the pertinent questions are not those that we as historians pose to the text but those questions the text poses to us as believers.

Once this stance is adopted, however, the problem is not solved. I may be eager to accept the words of Scripture as normative for my existence. But I still have not addressed the question of *how* those words are to be normative. Does Scripture stand before our reflection as a set of rules, which are clear in themselves though difficult to execute? Or does it provide us with a clear program of action regarding possessions, which must be translated, by structural analogy, to contemporary economic situations? Or is its testimony so diverse and historically conditioned that we must turn elsewhere for the right questions if not the right answers?

I declare that Scripture does provide us with the fundamental and normative framework for our thinking about the mystery of human possessing. I suggest that this framework is to be found not simply in the multiple mandates it presents but also, and more significantly, in its failure to present us with one clear and coherent program and its insistence that we recognize the importance of the disposition of possessions as a primordial symbol of human existence before God and in the world. In order to get to that perception, it will be helpful to start with a way of viewing possessions and the teaching of the Scriptures with which I do not agree, but which I think many people hold.

Comment

This introduction is more than a warm-up for the reader. It is an essential part of the book's argument. Much too often, Christians read Scripture for answers before they have really grappled with the nature of the question, or with the character of the texts from which they seek to learn. Stopping to think about the actual shape of the moral or religious question does not delay serious work; it enables and speeds it. Pausing to consider how Scripture asks to be approached when we seek norms for our contemporary life is not an academic distraction; it is critical to serious engagement with the texts. This part of my original introduction, then, could easily be extended — and readers passionately interested in the subject of the faithful use of possessions could best employ the remainder of the book by themselves pausing to consider the kind of questions I pose in this section.

Attention to the elusive language we inevitably deploy when speaking of "wealth and poverty" or "having and being" is imperative if we are to bring any degree of precision to our analysis either of life or of Scripture. Two points in my discussion of language I think deserve further emphasis.

The first is the way in which the terms "wealth" and "poverty" are relative to social context. The terms and their use are meaningful only within constantly shifting cultural realities and expectations. Wealth, for example, is measured by different means in different settings: in Botswana, for example, the possession of livestock is a more secure measure of wealth (in one's own and others' eyes) than the holding of stocks and bonds. In places where most people survive just above the level of starvation, wealth may mean having more than a day's rations. In places where most people have televisions, wealth may mean a communications center of unusual technical capacity. The measure of poverty is similarly contextual. The examples I just provided could simply be reversed: where wealth is cows, poverty is having none; where wealth is provender for two days, poverty is lacking more than a day's food; where wealth is a high-tech communications center, poverty can be an outdated television set.

The cultural context of language about poverty and wealth should caution us against using the terms in univocal and abstract ways. Establishing a "poverty line" in terms of money earned — in any context — is simply a way of trying to reduce a complex human mystery to the manageable dimensions of a "problem." In fact, however, a considerable amount of political and ecclesial talk about wealth and poverty uses language carelessly, without consideration for context. As a result, an air of unreality and ungrounded idealism suffuses many official and quasi-prophetic declarations.

The second aspect of language that I want to highlight from my earlier discussion is the way the claim to "have" and therefore to "be" extends beyond our bodies and our material possessions to every possible sort of "ownership," of ideas, plans, time, space, ideals, friends, partners, spouses, virtues. The point here must be made time and again: the mystery of being and having is not exhausted with a consideration of material things. Holding back or sharing generously at these other levels is deeply pertinent to the discussion of the faithful sharing of possessions.

The reason why language is so slippery, I suggest in this book, is that the reality itself is elusive, because it is rooted in the ambiguity of somatic-spiritual existence. Humans cannot escape "having," just as no amount of having can add anything to their "being." Recognizing such ambiguity helps us appreciate the difficulty of the subject, and the importance of starting with the body as symbol of the self. Because I both "am" and "have" a body, the disposition of my body and my possessions necessarily represents both the freedom of the spirit and the limitations of the body. No other attitude but humility is appropriate to the one who sets out to think through such matters.

The same humility is demanded in the consideration of how Scripture is to be read normatively. The treatment in this chapter is exceptionally brief. As I note in the epilogue, I pursue the entire question of scriptural authority for the church in my later book, *Scripture and Discernment: Decision Making in the Church.* What is said here, though, is of fundamental importance: first, the dominant mode of reading the Bible in the academy, the so-called historical-critical method, does not and cannot yield normativity; instead, it locks Scripture in the past. Some approach — here I call it reading with faith — other than historical is needed. In effect, we must read as though saying, "Speak, Lord, for your servant is listening." The second point, though, is equally important: Scripture does not necessarily yield its normative force at the level of command or mandate — its way of speaking normatively may be through another dimension of the text.

CHAPTER 1

Searching for a Mandate

W e want to take the Bible seriously as the norm for our Christian identity and action. How can we do this? To get our thinking started, I will begin with some propositions with which I do not agree but which are not uncommonly held. By digging away for a while at these propositions, we may begin to excavate the real question posed for us by the Scriptures.

The first proposition is that the Christian life, whatever else it may be, is surely a code of ethics. To be Christian means to live in one way and not another, to have certain definite values manifest themselves in certain definite patterns of behavior. What makes Christians different from others is the way they perceive and deal with life's important issues. The second proposition is that if this code of behavior is to have any consistency, and if the individual Christian is to know whether he or she is acting in a Christian manner, there must be a place where the appropriate ways of behaving are laid out. Where there is a code, we should be able to expect a codification. For Christians, this codification is found in the Bible, the Christian rulebook. The third proposition is that if the way people use money and possessions is at all significant for the Christian life, if the employment of material things is at all an ethical or religious issue, then this rulebook should have something clear and unambiguous to say about it. All we need to do to check whether our behavior is consonant with the Christian ethic is to consult the proper code.

Here, of course, is where we start to run into trouble. There is no lack of directives concerning the use of possessions in the Bible; they are everywhere. Nor is there any doubt that the Bible considers the use of material possessions significant for the life of faith. The problem is that the

11

directives seem to be saying different things: they seem to point us in different directions. When we face these conflicting demands squarely and refuse to harmonize them, we are forced to ask ourselves about our starting point. Is the Christian life a matter of a code of behavior? Is the Bible to be appropriated as a rulebook of behavior? Is what we do with material possessions really important for our Christian lives?

But is it really so difficult to derive a consistent mandate concerning the use of possessions from the Bible? I think it is, if we are really looking for a clear, consistent, and unequivocal direction for our behavior. In order to demonstrate this, I invite you to look with me at what is said in a single New Testament writing that is particularly replete with commands about possessions — Luke-Acts.

Luke-Acts is the shorthand title adopted by scholars for the two-volume work ordinarily called, respectively, the Gospel of Luke and the Acts of the Apostles. The title Luke-Acts indicates that although these writings appear separately in the canon, they were undoubtedly written by a first-century Christian teacher and historian as one continuous, though two-part, work. The first volume tells the story of Jesus; the second, the story of the beginning of the church. Both are told as the continuation of the biblical story of God's work among the chosen people through the prophets. The literary unity of Luke-Acts is important for the interpretation of this scriptural witness; to find out what Luke wished to teach on any particular subject, we must read Luke-Acts as a whole.

Even a cursory reading of Luke-Acts shows the author's concern about riches, poverty, and the use of possessions. References to these matters are more frequent in this Gospel than in any other. Luke has all the material on possessions found in Mark, and most of what is found in Matthew, with the exception of Matthew 5:5; 6:1-4; 13:44-45; 17:24-27; 18:23-35; 20:1-16; 25:31-46; and 27:3-10. Beyond this, there is a great deal of material dealing in one way or another with possessions which is unique to Luke, quite apart from what we find in Acts (see Luke 1:51-53; 3:10-14; 6:24; 8:1-3; 10:1-16; 10:38-42; 11:41; 12:13-21; 14:12-14; 15:8-10; 15:11-32; 16:1-9, 14, 19-31; 17:28-30, 32; 18:9-14; 19:1-10; 21:34-36; 22:35-38). Apart from 12:6 and 13:29, John's Gospel adds nothing to the synoptic tradition. So, in Luke, we have a compendium of the gospel teaching on possessions, and no end of attention has been paid to this "evangelist of the poor" by scholars. The trouble is that, after all this attention, scholars have a hard time deciding just *what* exactly Luke wants to teach his church (and, by extension, us) about the use of possessions. If we ask the simple and straightforward question posed by the hearers of John the Baptist, "What, then, are we to do?" (Luke 3:10), the answer is not altogether clear. Although Luke consistently speaks about possessions, he does not speak about possessions consistently. In what follows, I will deliberately isolate various strands within his text and refuse to harmonize them. I will, in effect, be treating Luke-Acts as a "code of Christian life," to see if we can follow Luke's directions concerning the use of possessions.

The Poor Are Privileged in the Eyes of God, and the Rich Condemned

In the beginning of the Gospel of Luke, when Mary praises God for the blessing of bearing the Messiah, she says, "he has filled the hungry with good things, and the rich he has sent empty away" (1:53). The sending away of the rich, together with the "scattering of the proud" and the putting down of the "mighty from their thrones" (1:51-52), is a sign of the reversal of fortunes and expectations brought about by God's visitation to his people (see 3:5-6; 14:11). The filling of the hungry with good things accompanies the exalting of "those of low degree" (1:52). The Greek word used for "those of low degree," *tapeinoi,* has definite resonances in the tradition. It designates not only those who are without possessions but those who are oppressed by their fellow human beings and must look to God for help, since they can expect none from elsewhere (for example, see Zeph. 2:3-9; 3:11-13; Isa. 25:4; 26:5-6; 28:5-6; 29:18-19; 41:17; 49:13; 61:1-4; 66:2; Jer. 20:13; Pss. 9:9, 12, 18; 10:14, 17-18; 12:5; 14:6; 22:24; 33:18-19; 34:6; 35:10; 36:7; 40:17; 55:22; 56:11; 62:1, 5-8; 68:5-6, 10; 69:32-33; 70:5; 71:4; 94:22; 102:17; 103:6; 124:8; 140:12; 146:7-9).

When Jesus starts his ministry, he applies to himself the reading from Isaiah 61:1-2, "The Spirit of the Lord is upon me, because he has anointed me to preach good news to the poor" (Luke 4:18). This is clearly intended to announce the kind of messiah Jesus was to be and the gist of his message. In his first major sermon, Jesus begins with a beatitude, "Blessed are you poor, for yours is the kingdom of God" (6:20). We notice that this is not moralistically shaded, as is Matthew 5:3, "Blessed are the poor in spirit, for theirs is the kingdom of heaven." No, Luke says "you poor," as though the group of disciples and others who heard him (6:17, 20) were themselves poor. And the word "poor" seems to bear its usual meaning of being without material goods. Jesus calls such as these blessed, simply because the good news is addressed to them. Lest we miss the point, Luke alone has added to his beatitudes a series of woes, the first of which reads, "woe to you that are rich, for you have received your consolation" (6:24).

The division established by the beatitude and woe continues throughout Luke's Gospel. When John the Baptist sends messengers to ask whether Jesus is the awaited Messiah, Jesus' response has as its climax the notice that "the poor have good news preached to them" (7:22). The program of prophetic visitation enunciated at 4:18 and announced at 6:20 is here certified by the work of Jesus. The call of the poor to God's kingdom is also signaled by the parable of the banquet that Jesus told while sitting in the house of a Pharisee (14:16-24). Those who were first invited to the banquet refused the invitation because they were too involved with the affairs of their lives to respond (14:18-20). More about them later. The master grew angry and sent his servants to bring into the banquet "the poor and maimed and blind and lame" (14:21). As the poor stood in last place at 7:22, here they stand first in line, representing those outcast from the people Israel whom God calls to his feast. This parable, in turn, serves as the model for human hospitality: "when you give a feast, invite the poor, the maimed, the lame, the blind, and you will be blessed, because they cannot repay you" (14:13-14).

The blessing of the poor and the rejection of the rich by God is sharply expressed in the story of Lazarus and the rich man (16:19-31) told to certain Pharisees, whom Luke calls "lovers of money" (16:14), who had scoffed at Jesus' words about loving God more than money. The story captures precisely the import of the first beatitude and woe found in Luke. We are not told explicitly that the rich man did anything bad in his lifetime (though from 16:19 and 31 the implication might be drawn that he did not practice alms); he was just exceptionally rich. He had his consolation in this life (see 6:24) and after death had to sit in Hades, bereft of comfort. Nor are we told that Lazarus was particularly virtuous. He was simply miserably poor in this life, and in the next life received his consolation, apparently for that reason alone (16:25).

Let us pause for a moment and consider what the implications of passages such as these might be, if we take them in isolation and apply them to our lives as norms. We note immediately that these are not passages about how one should use possessions, but passages about how God views people who have or do not have a certain amount of possessions. Clearly, God loves the poor and hates the rich. Otherwise, why is

God's good news directed to the poor as a blessing and heard by the rich only as a woe? Otherwise, why punish a man simply because he is rich and reward another simply because he is poor?

And what are the implications of this for me? Does it mean that if I have a great deal of money or property the good news is not for me? If I am rich, am I automatically excluded from God's care? But, then, what does it mean to be "rich"? What exactly is the measure? How much property or money does it take? This is not a trivial question if God favors those below a certain economic line and detests those above it. Is wealth determined by the quantity of material things I have or the degree of my attachment to them? Or is there something evil about possessions as such that taints everyone to some degree, and more when more is owned? Another question is whether being rich or poor is an absolute or relative state. Are there degrees of richness and poverty, and do these degrees indicate relative position within or without God's people or God's favor? If so, once again, what is the measure? Must I divest myself of all I own and become destitute, or only become uncomfortable? Do I have to live in a hovel, or only a second-class hotel? These are all grim questions and not easy to resolve. Not only are we puzzled by what appears to be a decided selectivity in God's mercy, but also by the vagueness of the conditions under which we might confidently expect that mercy.

Jesus Demands Complete Renunciation
of Possessions for Disciples

Luke makes a point of noting that, when Jesus called his first disciples, "they left everything and followed him" (5:11). Levi the tax collector also, when called by Jesus, "left everything . . . and followed him" (5:28). The tax collector left a lucrative sinecure; Peter and the sons of Zebedee left their source of livelihood. Peter later had occasion to remind Jesus of this. That occasion was when the rich ruler came and asked Jesus what he should do to inherit eternal life (18:18). Jesus' first response was that the man should keep the commandments. When the ruler said he had already done that, Jesus told him, "Sell all that you have and distribute to the poor, and you will have treasure in heaven; and come, follow me" (18:22). The man withdrew sadly, for, as Luke notes, "he was very rich" (18:23). Jesus' comment on the whole situation was that it would be easier for a camel to pass through the eye of a needle than for a rich man to enter the kingdom of God (18:24-25). This encounter and Jesus' interpretation threw his hearers into consternation: "Why, then, who can be saved?" Jesus assures them that what is impossible with human resources is possible by God's power (suggesting a way open to the rich?). When Peter reminds Jesus that he and the Zebedee brothers had in fact left their own things in order to follow him (18:28), Jesus promises a reward in this life and in the next (18:29-30). If we read this story "on the flat," we can gain no other impression than that just as the first disciples left everything to follow Jesus, and could therefore look for a reward, so this is expected of any subsequent follower. Beyond keeping the commandments, they must sell all they have and become destitute followers of the Messiah. The rich man in the story simply failed to meet this demand of discipleship and was therefore rejected.

The same point is forcefully made in the passage following the parable of the great banquet in chapter 14, in which, as we saw, those first invited refused to come. In 14:25ff., Jesus turns to the great multitudes following him and states the demands of discipleship. Disciples must be willing to leave behind all close relationships and to take up their cross after him (14:25-27). He warns them to count the cost before responding (14:28-32) and concludes with this unequivocal demand regarding possessions: "whoever of you does not renounce all that he has cannot be my disciple" (14:33).

Now, this is consistent enough and follows logically from the first theme: that God's good news is for the poor and not for the rich. By stripping ourselves of all our possessions and becoming destitute, we place ourselves among the "poor" and can therefore both receive and respond to God's invitation to the kingdom. If we take these sayings of Jesus as being addressed to us as "disciples," there does not seem to be any way of avoiding the demand — being a follower of Jesus demands becoming radically poor. The question that needs to be asked now is whether this demand was made of all those who accepted Jesus as the Messiah in the Gospel story.

Disciples of Jesus Are to Give Alms
to Help the Poor and Provide Hospitality

There is another way of using possessions mentioned in Luke-Acts, which is perhaps the dominant response called for — that practice of "charity" or "justice" called almsgiving. The ideal of almsgiving seems at least to be implied in the difficult story of the unjust steward and its awkwardly appended sayings about mammon (16:1-13). Jesus expressed admiration for the cunning, if not the morality, of the rich man's steward who, when caught fiddling with the books, secured a place for himself among his master's debtors by still more financial fiddling. Jesus recommends to his followers that they show similar enterprise in their response to crisis. The second moral of the story addresses more directly the use of possessions by the disciples: "make friends for yourselves by means of unrighteous mammon, so that when it fails they may receive you into the eternal habitations" (16:9). If we attach this moral to the pattern of the story, this would mean that the disciples are to use money in a way that will secure them a reward from God; as the steward found a place, in effect, by distributing goods among the creditors, so they will find a place in heaven by the distribution of alms (16:10-13). The sayings that follow are notoriously obscure. In each, a lesser activity or reality is contrasted with a greater one. What seems clear from this passage is that the followers of Jesus are expected to use their possessions in a creative way (see also 19:11-27); they are to give alms to the poor, and this will secure them a place in heaven. We notice the similarity to that which was told the rich ruler in 18:22. He was to have a treasure in heaven if he sold what he had and gave it to the poor. The difference, of course, is that the rich ruler was expected to sell all he had, and here there is no hint of that.

In another place (12:33), after a long series of passages dealing with possessions, to which we shall return, Jesus tells those who have already become his disciples, "Sell your possessions, and give alms; provide yourselves with purses that do not grow old, with a treasure in the heavens that does not fail. . . ." We see immediately the recurrence of the treasure in heaven motif. We also notice that those who are already disciples (see 12:22) and presumably had left all to follow Jesus are now presumed able to give alms. Here there is clearly no requirement to sell all they have.

In an extended attack on the Pharisees and lawyers (11:37-52), Jesus tells them to "give alms for those things which are within; and behold, everything is clean for you" (11:41). This is rather strangely put, but it is clear that almsgiving is contrasted positively with the obsessive concern with ritual purity of which Jesus accuses his opponents. Almsgiving makes another appearance in the Gospel narrative in the story of the widow's offering in 21:1-4. The widow put two copper coins into the treasury, whereas the rich people put in great amounts of money. The setting here is not entirely clear, nor is the action. I suspect that what Luke had Jesus observing was the giving of money into the "chamber of secrets" in the temple, a predecessor of the poor fund in Jewish organized charity, from which the poor might secretly draw what they needed. The woman who put in the small coins, therefore, was practicing almsgiving. The widow is said to have given more than all the rich, for they gave out of their abundance, but she out of her subsistence (21:4). Jesus by no means condemns the rich who put in great amounts of money; the generosity of the woman is only heightened in contrast to theirs. It can also be mentioned that this woman was not said to be a follower of Jesus.

The practice of almsgiving is found also in Acts, where, strangely, the contrast between rich and poor, so sharply defined in the Gospel, is entirely lacking. The woman Tabitha is said to have been "full of good works and acts of charity" (that is, almsgiving, 9:36). The centurion Cornelius was one who "feared God with all his household, gave alms liberally to the people, and prayed constantly to God" (Acts 10:2). Cornelius is told by God in a vision that his "prayers and . . . alms have ascended as a memorial before God" (10:4).

When we turn back to the Gospel, and look at the narrative rather than at directives, we see that not all those who believed in Jesus sold everything they had in response. In Luke 8:1-3, brief mention is made of a group of women who were traveling through Galilee with Jesus and the disciples, and who "provided for them out of their means." These are the same women who followed Jesus all the way to the cross and who made up part of the nucleus of the restored people. There is no question that they followed Jesus. Rather than give away their possessions, however, they used them to support the ministry of Jesus and the Twelve.

The diminutive Zacchaeus who was so eager to see Jesus also happened to be a chief tax collector and very rich (Luke 19:2). When he welcomed Jesus into his house, he promised to give half his possessions to the poor and repay fourfold to any he had defrauded in the course of tax collecting (19:8). This is an extraordinarily generous response, it is true, but not absolute renunciation. Yet, Jesus said, "Today salvation has come to this house, since he also is a son of Abraham" (19:9). We are not told that he sold his house, left all his possessions, and followed Jesus, or even that he stopped being a tax collector. There is no implication that he ceased being "rich." Half a bundle may still, after all, be a bundle. By giving alms to the poor, and by restoring what he had taken, and above all by providing hospitality to the Messiah, Zacchaeus showed himself to be a "son of Abraham." In this, he was much like those intriguing sisters Martha and Mary (Luke 10:38-42), who likewise received Jesus into their house, each with a different style of hospitality. They did not, so far as we know, subsequently sell that house and follow Jesus, nor was this demanded of them. Throughout Luke-Acts, hospitality shown to the emissaries of God is a sign of acceptance and faith (see also Luke 9:3-5; 9:53; 10:5-12, 16; 14:12-14; 24:28-32; Acts 10:23-33; 16:14-15, 32-34; 28:1-2, 7-10). This expressive character of hospitality is what makes the false hospitality of the Pharisees so shocking, when they have Jesus in their houses, but use the occasion to test him (Luke 7:36-50; 14:1-6).

Side by side with the call to total renunciation of possessions, therefore, we find the ideal of almsgiving and hospitality. A simple but important point must be made about this. If the two practices are not mutually exclusive, they are at least impossible to practice at one and the same time. What are the possibilities? If I am already among the "poor," or destitute, I simply do not have the means to give alms, unless, like the poor widow, I give "all my living." If I have possessions, and sell them all in order to be a disciple, this can indeed be seen as a form of almsgiving, but if I really sell "all," then I too enter the ranks of the destitute, no longer able to give alms, but to rely on the alms and generosity of others who have held on to their possessions. My almsgiving, if so it can be called, is of a once-for-all nature. To give alms on a continuing basis, one must have something to give; one must maintain some possessions. To provide hospitality to the needy and wandering, one needs to have a house, or at least a room.

Christians Must Hold All Their Possessions in Common

The ideal of holding possessions in common is expressed in only one part of Luke-Acts, in the portrait Luke draws of the primitive Christian community in Jerusalem after Pentecost. In Acts 2:44-45, he notes briefly that "all who believed were together and had all things in common; and they sold their possessions and goods and distributed them to all, as any had need." In 4:32-35, there is a longer description, which stresses the spiritual unity of the community (they "were of one heart and soul"), the role of the apostles in the practice (the believers "brought the proceeds of what was sold and laid it at the apostles' feet; and distribution was made to each as any had need"), and the success of the venture ("there was not a needy person among them"). Here, then, we have a third demand concerning the use of possessions. The disciples are not completely destitute or poor, for "there was not a needy person among them," and in any community of goods there is "use" by all. Nor is this strictly a form of almsgiving, for almsgiving requires something that one can call "one's own" to give. Here, there is the complete pooling of property ("they had everything in common"), and the relinquishment of private ownership ("no one said that any of the things which he possessed was his own").

As isolated as it is in the Acts narrative, this community of goods is described as a serious affair. Although the donation of goods appears to have been voluntary (5:4), Ananias and Sapphira, who faked a participation in the practice, were struck dead (5:1-11). On the other hand, on the strength of the textual evidence itself, the practice seems to have been less than absolute. Peter, after all, has a house to flee to when he escapes from prison (12:12), and if the Christians were "breaking bread in their homes" (2:46), some houses obviously were retained in possession. It is also puzzling why, if the sharing was so successful, the Jerusalem community fell so quickly into trouble at the time of the famine and required help from the Antiochian church. In Acts 11:27-30 we read that the brothers in that city took up a collection to send to the needy in Judea. There is no suggestion that there was a community fund in Antioch out of which the collection could be drawn, or that the motivation was that all Christians were "one heart and soul." Indeed, each Antiochian contributed "according to his ability," which indicates the existence of not only private possessions but differences in wealth (11:29). The whole affair sounds more like almsgiving than a community of goods in the strict sense.

In chapter 4 I will return to the question of how and why Luke was idealizing this practice, and to what extent he may have intended it to stand as a model for other churches to imitate. It is important to recognize, however, that whatever Luke's intentions, this text has been taken as a mandate or at least a model by many communities throughout the history of Christianity. Given this, it is also important to acknowledge that, just as the theme of the rich and the poor is dropped midway through the Gospel, never to reappear, so also this description of a community of goods is found only here, and although Luke had other opportunities to exploit the motif of sharing in this way, he never did so.

It bears repeating that there is at least a logical tension between the ideals of wandering destitution, almsgiving, hospitality, and a community of goods. In a community of goods, as I have mentioned, there is a relinquishment of ownership, and therefore of personal disposition. A community as a whole can give "alms," but no individual within the community can, as an individual. Furthermore, a community of goods exists for the support and sustenance of those within the community, not outsiders. Almsgiving, on the other hand, is at least potentially open to anyone in need. When Peter and John were confronted by the beggar at the Beautiful Gate and asked for alms (which Peter should have been able to give since he held the purse, according to Acts 4:32ff.), Peter responded, "I have no silver and gold, but I give you what I have; in the name of Jesus Christ of Nazareth, walk" (Acts 3:6). This is not by any means a bad replacement! But it shows the tension between community possessions and almsgiving. To say that the first is an exemplification of the second is simply inaccurate. Anyone who has taken the trouble to go through all of Luke-Acts must have been bothered by this diversity of mandates regarding possessions. As could be expected, there have been multiple explanations for the diversities and tensions. Some argue for a mix of traditions awkwardly joined (unlikely in a writer as careful as Luke). Some say that the tensions point to different demands for different periods (destitution for the time of Jesus, community of goods for the time of the church), or different demands for different people in the church (the radical demands for ministers, almsgiving for the lay folk). These and other ingenious suggestions try to put some systematic unity on the diversity. But not only do these solutions not work on their own grounds (of historical criticism), they mean little to anyone not possessing a sophisticated method for bringing consistency to what is plainly inconsistent. For the sake of exposing just a bit more of that inconsistency, however, let us follow up on the last suggestion, for it is, after all, an attractive thesis — that ministers and spiritual leaders in the church should be held to a higher standard regarding possessions than people who have to work for a living.

Christian Ministers Are/Are Not
to Travel and Work Without Possessions

We have already seen how those first called by Jesus to follow him left behind everything (although Levi managed to provide for Jesus "a great feast in his house," Luke 5:29). When Jesus commissions the Twelve to preach the good news and heal (9:3ff.) he tells them, "Take nothing for your journey, no staff, nor bag, nor bread, nor money; and do not have two tunics." This is a fairly complete inventory. They are to go out unprovisioned and depend on the hospitality of those willing to receive them and the word of the gospel (9:4-5). Much the same sort of thing is told the seventy(-two) when they are sent on ahead of Jesus on his trip to Jerusalem to prepare his way (10:3ff.). Again, "no purse, no bag, no sandals"; and again, they are to depend on the hospitality of others, for "the laborer deserves his wages" (10:7). It seems pretty clear that Jesus wishes his missionaries to travel about in this fashion. But here is a strange thing. In Luke's account of the Last Supper, we hear Jesus asking the Twelve, "When I sent you out with no purse or bag or sandals, did you lack anything?" They answer that they had not. Then he tells them, "But now, let him who has a purse take it, and likewise a bag. And let him who has no sword sell his mantle and buy one" (22:35-36). This is a difficult passage on many counts. For one thing, Luke has Jesus ask a question of the Twelve in terms that would have been more appropriate to the seventy(-two). But as for the use of possessions, the passage is rather straightforward. The earlier command of Jesus is revoked; his followers are now to travel with provisions.

When we turn to the picture of the leaders and missionaries in the Acts of the Apostles, the evidence concerning possessions is no less diverse. We have already seen how Peter had no silver or gold to give the beggar (3:6). Yet, as one of the Twelve, he was over the community of possessions and distributed the goods to whoever had need (4:35). Now we find another abrupt shift. In 6:1ff., the apostles state that the administrative burden has interfered with their prayer and preaching, so they hand it over to another group, the Seven. The Seven then go off and preach and teach just as the Twelve had, and we hear nothing more about their handling the distribution of the community's goods.

The preachers in Acts who best fit the image of Luke 9:1ff. and 10:1ff. are Paul and Barnabas. In fact, they explicitly fulfill one of the missionary commands of Jesus (Luke 10:11) by shaking the dust off their feet when rejected by the Jews of Antioch of Pisidia (Acts 13:51). But there is no mention of them traveling without provisions. In fact, Paul is said to have worked for a living (18:3). In 21:24, when Paul comes to Jerusalem, he has sufficient pocket money to pay the temple fees for himself and four others. There is an intriguing note in 24:26, especially since Luke strangely says nothing at all about a Pauline collection. While Paul was in prison in Caesarea, Felix, his captor, hoped to get a bribe from Paul, for he knew that he had a large sum of money with him. When under house arrest in Rome, Paul stayed in his own rented dwelling (28:30). Finally, when Paul addresses the elders of the Ephesian church at Miletus, he holds up to them his own example regarding the use of possessions. Far from being a wandering mendicant, dependent on his communities, he made no demands on anyone. Indeed, he worked with his own hands. He not only met his own needs by his own labor, but he earned enough to help others more needy. He tells the elders that they should act in this way as well. In accordance with the saying of the Lord, "It is more blessed to give than to receive" (Acts 20:18-35).

Faced with this multiplicity of models and mandates for those who are explicitly pictured as leaders of the church, which are we to regard as normative? Are Christian ministers to be wandering beggars, relying on the hospitality of others? Are they to carry their own provisions and a sword besides? Are they to administer the community's shared resources? Are they to work at a job for their own support, and thereby be able to support others as well? At the level of directive, it should be abundantly clear that Luke is not clear.

I trust that by now my reader is sufficiently confused. I have not deliberately obscured the issues, but have simply tried to avoid harmonizing them too quickly. Exposure to the complexity of this material is imperative if we are to find a way of understanding what Luke or any of the biblical writers are trying to teach us about the significance of possessions for the Christian life. It is terribly difficult, I think, for the Christian who takes the Bible seriously and regards it as providing guidance for daily life, to find a clear-cut, concrete directive that can be followed consistently. To be a real Christian, must I be poor, join a commune, or make enough money to give alms? Should I seek in my ministers a radical poverty, an administrative hand, or a worker-priest?

You may already be having doubts about the extent to which we can use the Scriptures as a rulebook for this aspect of the Christian life. And the complexity of directives in Luke-Acts is only a small portion of the mandates we can find in the Old and New Testaments as a whole. But before we too quickly seek a resolution to these doubts, let us press the logic of our quest a bit further. It is important to do this occasionally, for if there is one thing many of us secretly would like to get out of the Scriptures, it is a rulebook.

We know that rules are valid only insofar as they are absolute. This is the basis both of games and of civilization. In baseball, a ball hit to the same spot twice successively cannot be fair one inning and foul the next, or fair for one player and foul for another. In wrestling, kicking and gouging cannot be fair for one and foul for the other wrestler. Assault cannot be all right for me but not for you.

But what do we do when we are confronted with what seem to be conflicting if not contradictory rules? We have three options: (1) We can say that one rule (because it is better, fairer, or whatever) is more binding than another. That is, we can be selective. In effect, this means making one rule binding and the others not. (2) We can say that such self-contradiction makes all the rules relative, and therefore none applies. (3) We can begin to ask whether this is a rulebook we are dealing with in the first place.

Historically, it seems, most Christians have taken the Bible seriously as a set of directives and have exercised the option of selectivity regarding the use of possessions. For some, to be a "real Christian" has meant, in one form or another, to be radically poor. This was the response of the first hermits, such as Anthony. In the high Middle Ages, mendicancy, both with and without orthodoxy, was considered the more perfect way of being Christian (the tendency to regard what is more spectacular as better is very old). Not only does this option tend to create a kind of spiritual elitism, as can be seen by perusing any treatment of the "states of perfection," but the mendicant must deal with the paradox that his or her life of perfect poverty depends on the existence of people willing to support the beggar — generally Christians of lesser spiritual nobility but with jobs, who can offer alms and hospitality to those more saintly.

Many others became monks of one sort or another and shared all their possessions in common. The myth that monks were the true inheritors of the primitive Christian zeal and lifestyle came early and stayed late, and monks always looked to Acts 2 and 4 for the explicit legitimation for their community of goods (more on this in chapter 4). The monastic option has the advantage of enabling the individual monk to be perfectly poor (not even having his own body at his disposal, the Rule of Benedict says) while enjoying extraordinary security from the vicissitudes of profane life. Monks, too, have a paradox to live with: the logic of their practice leads inevitably to people who are "spiritually poor" living within increasingly wealthy institutions.

The monastic way was explicitly rejected by some of the major leaders of the Protestant Reformation, especially Calvin and Luther. But some Anabaptist groups seized upon the ideal of community possessions with an egalitarian fervor. The city of Münster, which in the sixteenth century became briefly the New Jerusalem under John of Leiden, was the supreme example. In that unhappy and apocalyptic experiment, people found that the common goods were more common to some than to others, and that while the populace became increasingly and involuntarily poor, the leaders became increasingly and aggressively wealthy. This pattern has recurred. In recent years, the People's Temple under Jim Jones, a movement that came to a grisly end in the jungle of Guyana, demonstrated the lesson of this sort of sharing in the picture of a locked trunk full of passports. There continue to be less flamboyant forms of community possessions both within and without Christianity, whether in communes or communities. Almost inevitably such movements look to the words of Jesus or the Acts of the Apostles for their legitimation. Almost inevitably, the practice leads to a distinct air of superiority.

There has also been another form of selectivity. Some have considered almsgiving to be the only legitimate manifestation of the Christian ideal. Those who have made this selection have also usually recognized the logic of almsgiving and pursued it with admirable consistency. To give alms, one must own things, preferably liquid assets. It follows that, to give alms in a really impressive fashion, one should have a great deal of capital. The first task, therefore, is to set about collecting as much potential alms as possible. This is the "need to be a capitalist in order to be a philanthropist" syndrome. Unfortunately, the process of acquiring has almost always proven to be more fascinating than the process of dispersing. Philanthropists of the classic stripe have had their paradox too: that of returning to others through largesse what was taken from them in the first place by greed.

The majority of ordinary people who wish to be Christian (among whom I include myself) probably find themselves operating, willy-nilly, within the second option. We are vaguely aware of the multiple demands concerning possessions in the Scriptures (though we may not have seen how multiple or how contradictory). But these demands not only seem to cancel each other out; they also appear incapable of being fulfilled in this complex contemporary world.

How can I form a community of goods and remain a citizen of the modern city? Must Christianity in its best form inevitably be rural? To be Christian, must I go to a monastery or ashram? On the other hand, how can I give alms when I can barely support my family, not in luxury, but in shoes? Tithing may help the church, but does it have any impact on the state of the destitute? And if I contribute to the United Way or some other organized charity, how much gets to the poor and how much supports the bureaucracy of the organization? What about radical options? Are the only real Christians those living at Clarence Jordan's Koinonia Farm, or Dorothy Day's Catholic Worker, or Ann Arbor's Word of God community, or one of the Bruderhof communities? Outside such an intentional community, how can one be destitute "for the Lord," when, in our society, this means either going on welfare or relying on the generosity of other Christians who are themselves financially hard-pressed? How can possessions be used in any sanctified way in a world governed, not by barter, not by real goods, not even by stable currencies, but by the intricacies of manipulations by cartels, of shifting interest rates, computer credit ratings, conglomerates, and international monetary fluctuations?

Faced, on the one hand, with what appears to be the inapplicability of the biblical directives as rules and, on the other, with the sheer complexity and difficulty of economic survival in a world caught in the downward spiral of diminishing resources and the upward spiral of inflation, many of us may despair of bringing this aspect of our existence in any way within the frame of our self-understanding as Christians. We may feel vaguely guilty: surely something important lies behind so many mandates. But we also feel unable to figure out what this is. Is there any alternative to muddling? I think so. I consider it possible both to take the Bible seriously in what it says about possessions and not to regard it as a set of rules. But how?

Comment

I tried in this chapter to challenge the all-too-common assumption that, if we accept that the Bible is normative for life, then it must be easy to determine what that norm is. It is just a matter of careful reading. To the contrary, I argue, the more carefully we read, the more complex the question of norms becomes and the more difficult it is to determine just how Scripture speaks normatively. So, I did nothing more complicated than to treat each mandate found in Luke-Acts with full seriousness, showing that it is logically impossible to obey all of the mandates without falling into contradiction.

Quite unconsciously, I was employing an approach frequently used by the church's first great Scripture scholar, Origen of Alexandria. Origen was fond of pushing the literal sense of Scripture to its limits, precisely to demonstrate the need to shift to another dimension of reading, what he called the "anagogical level." He was convinced, as we should be, that God speaks to us through these texts and seeks to instruct us wisely in each of them. Our task is to discover the *mode* in which God addresses us. Origen was convinced that this was not always, or even most importantly, at the level of the literal narrative or the literal commandment. Thus, he would take a prescription for humans or a description of God found in Scripture and demonstrate how, if taken literally, one would end up being a Jew (observing the ritual laws of Torah) or a Marcionite (despising the God of Israel because of the traits ascribed to him). Origen would follow the same practice with respect to the New Testament, showing, for example, how the differences among the Gospel narratives called for a manner of reading that did not demand of Jesus that he say or do self-contradictory things. In short, Origen sought to create in his readers an *aporia* from which only an anagogical (spiritual) reading would deliver them.

Although my critical instincts in this chapter had ancient antecedents, my constructive instincts show me to be thoroughly modern. I do not, like Origen, seek God's wisdom in an anagogical reading that addresses the soul rather than the body, dealing with mystical rather than physical realities, but I remain thoroughly within the range of the literal meaning of the text and the somatic character of human existence. I simply shift attention, in the next chapter, to the human responses to God respectively of idolatry and faith — each of which has specific somatic expressions, each of which is symbolized by the disposition of possessions. My shift is from the level of command to the level of symbol. I was and am convinced that only when we recognize the symbolic character of possessions within the fundamental anthropological responses to God of rebellion and obedience, are we in a position to revisit and assess the force of the various mandates.

Some readers might have concluded, from my rapid survey of the ways in which Christians through the ages selected one mandate as normative rather than another, that I somehow despised their efforts. Such was far from my intention. Indeed, the efforts to fulfill the mandates through voluntary poverty, living within a community of goods, almsgiving, and working to support others all deserve respect, and all in some manner correspond to Scripture. My intention, rather, was to make two points. The first is that none of these modes of sharing material possessions exhausts the most profound theological mandate of sharing all that we claim to own as an expression of faith. The second is that each of these modes can be a legitimate expression of sharing material possessions, even as none of them fully expresses faith's demand to share with others all that we claim to have.

There is yet a third point, which is particularly important to make in the present ecclesial climate, especially in the United States. It can be stated unequivocally that Luke-Acts — the scriptural witness that speaks most emphatically about the human use of possessions as a response of faith — bears no trace of the contemporary heresy called the prosperity gospel. However much televangelists and others trumpet the "scriptural" character of their claim that faith brings with it material prosperity, their selectivity with regard to the Bible is far more severe than that practiced by Christians who have followed one of the classic options for sharing. They choose to follow a handful of Old Testament texts in the Deuteronomic tradition, and ignore completely the unanimous witness of the New Testament, which portrays discipleship not in terms of worldly success, but in terms of radical obedience and service — service that involves the sharing of possessions rather than the accumulation of them. There is simply no gospel character to the claims of the prosperity gospel, no element of genuine Christian discipleship.

CHAPTER 2

Toward a Theological Understanding of Possessions

O ur attempt to find in Luke-Acts a clear code of behavior for the Christian use of possessions was flawed not only because of the diversity of mandates found in that writing but, more significantly, because the attempt was generated by a false understanding of the nature of Christian existence. The proposition with which I started is simply false: Christianity is not, first of all, a form of ethics or code of behavior. Prior to any actions or pattern of actions we might term "Christian" is a whole set of perceptions and attitudes, which themselves emerge from a coherent system of symbols, and an orientation toward the world and other humans, which we call Faith. Ideally, a Christian's actions emerge with some degree of consistency from these perceptions and attitudes. We know that if we want to discern the Christian character of our behavior, we must first look to the motivations that impel our actions. We are aware, with Thomas Becket in T. S. Eliot's *Murder in the Cathedral,* that the last and greatest treason may be to do the right things for the wrong reason. We are convinced that our identity is found in our inner heart, where we desire and will, and that God, the discerner of hearts, looks not so much to our actions as to our intentions.

It may be pertinent to ask, however, if this Christian identity is totally a matter of the inner heart, so locked up in the recesses of interiority that it is never expressed externally. Is there a complete and unbridgeable gap between our inner and outer selves? Of course not. But we need to ask about the connection between the two: How do we get from "in here" to "out there" with any consistency? We have learned from the Gospels that it is possible to camouflage the inner state by outer action, with hypocrisy. But hypocrisy gains its destructive power only by its distortion of the

truth about the connection between the hearts of people and their actions: that out of the heart's fullness the mouth speaks; that from a good
tree good fruit will come forth (Matt. 7:17-18). If our bodily actions did not
reveal our inner selves, hypocrisy would have no sting to its perversion.

Body and Symbol

If we are to have any hope of reading the Scriptures as addressed to our
experience of owning and having, we must begin by paying attention to
this connection between the inner and outer person, a connection that
Scripture itself never loses sight of. The Bible bears witness everywhere
that we humans are symbolic creatures, whose attitudes and convictions
are expressed in the language of the body. To remind us of this, and to
stimulate our imagination a bit, I would like to remind you of just how
pervasive this perception of "body language" is in the Scriptures. As I
touch upon this or that passage in a rapid run through the texts, I hope
that your imagination begins to form concrete images of how the body
speaks in each case. In this situation above all, theology must begin with
the controlled and creative fantasy of the imagination. As the figures of
our story pass before our minds, we might think how they place their
bodies in statement, protest, assertion, question, or plea, and how a
stick, a garment, or a sword can extend that language.

When Adam and Eve discovered their nakedness and heard the
sound of the Lord God walking in the garden in the cool of the evening,
they hid in the trees. Adam told God, "I heard the sound of thee in the
garden, and I was afraid, because I was naked; and I hid myself" (Gen.
3:8-10). Abraham bowed to the earth before the three men who came to
his tent (Gen. 18:2); Abraham's servant swore to his master by putting his
hand "under Abraham's thigh" (Gen. 24:9); Jacob crossed his right and
left hands when laying them on the heads of Manasseh and Ephraim to
signify which would be greater (Gen. 48:14); Moses stretched out his
hand over the sea (Exod. 14:21), held out his arm over Amalek in battle
(Exod. 17:11), and struck the rock with his rod (Num. 20:11); Joshua told
the men of Israel at the capture of the five kings to "put your feet upon
the necks of these kings," and then said, "thus the Lord will do to all your
enemies against whom you fight" (Josh. 10:24-25).

The Levite whose concubine was raped and murdered by the men of
Gibeah cut her body into twelve pieces and sent them through the terri-

tory of Israel as a summons to vengeance (Judg. 19:29); when Saul tore Samuel's robe, Samuel said, "The Lord has torn the kingdom of Israel from you this day" (1 Sam. 15:27-28); Ahijah tore his own garment into twelve pieces and said to Jeroboam, "Take for yourself ten pieces; for thus says the Lord, the God of Israel, 'Behold, I am about to tear the kingdom from the hand of Solomon, and will give you ten tribes'" (1 Kings 11:30-31).

Elijah stretched himself over the dead child of the widow of Zarephath three times and cried to the Lord, "O Lord my God, let this child's soul come into him again" (1 Kings 17:21); and after Elijah heard the still small voice on the mountain of the Lord, he "wrapped his face in his mantle" (1 Kings 19:13). Elisha, too, raised a dead child, "putting his mouth upon his mouth, his eyes upon his eyes, and his hands upon his hands," and when he rose up, the child sneezed seven times and opened his eyes, and Elisha said, "call this Shunammite," and to her, "Take up your son." She, in turn, "fell at his feet, bowing to the ground" (2 Kings 4:32-37). So had the beautiful Abigail fallen at David's feet, saying, "Upon me alone, my Lord, be the guilt" (1 Sam. 25:24); and David himself "danced before the Lord with all his might" (2 Sam. 6:14).

Jeremiah buried a soiled waistband by the bank of the Euphrates, and when he dug it up and saw it was spoiled, prophesied, "Thus says the Lord: Even so will I spoil the pride of Judah and the great pride of Jerusalem" (Jer. 13:1-9). Jeremiah also, when the city was under siege by the Chaldeans, bought a field in Anathoth with great and legal ceremony, saying, "Thus says the Lord of hosts, the God of Israel: Houses and fields and vineyards shall again be bought in this land" (Jer. 32:6-15). Ezekiel the prophet lay on his side bound with cords, before a model of Jerusalem besieged; ate the food of fasting; cut his hair in batches, burning some, striking some with the sword, and scattering some to the wind; thus he symbolized with his body the disaster befalling Jerusalem (Ezek. 4:1–5:12). And he clapped his hands and stamped his foot, and said, "Alas! because of all the evil abominations of the house of Israel" (Ezek. 6:11). Ezekiel presented his body to the people as a symbol of God's Word, "I am a sign for you" (Ezek. 12:11). So had the prophet Hosea spoken God's Word with his body when at the Lord's bidding he took a harlot to be his wife, "for the land commits great harlotry by forsaking the Lord" (Hos. 1:2).

In this fashion, too, did God speak when Jesus touched the ears and tongue of the deaf-mute man (Mark 7:33) and the eyes of the blind man (Mark 8:22-26); made the leper clean by touching him (Mark 1:41); ate with tax collectors and sinners (Luke 5:30); held little children in his arms (Mark 10:16); and, at his last meal with his chosen friends, "took bread, and blessed, and broke it, and gave it to them and said, 'Take; this is my body'" (Mark 14:22).

Research into psychosomatic medicine, and the analysis of games, rituals, and body language of every sort remind us of what the better part of Western philosophy for some centuries has been trying to make us forget: that human beings are not minds that are more or less harnessed to, or harnessing, machines, but that the intricate interworkings of soul and body are profound, mysterious, and undeniably real. Early psychoanalytic study showed the connection between states of hysteria and paralysis, between anger and catatonia. More recent study has shown an even wider range of psychogenetic disorders, even in cases of organic disease. It has also indicated that the traffic moves both ways: the body's condition and the mix of chemicals washing through our systems have the most shocking and evident repercussions on our states of elation and despair. Not with the insights of endocrinology, but with the acute observation of real people gripped by fear, pain, anger, and joy, the writers of the biblical narratives spoke out of the same perception, no less truly if with naiveté: "an evil spirit from God rushed upon Saul, and he raved within his house, while David was playing the lyre, as he did day by day. Saul had his spear in his hand; and Saul cast the spear, for he thought, 'I will pin David to the wall'" (1 Sam. 18:10-11); "there met him out of the tombs a man with an unclean spirit . . . no one could bind him any more, even with a chain . . . no one had the strength to subdue him. . . . And they came to Jesus, and saw the demoniac sitting there, clothed and in his right mind, the man who had had the legion; and they were afraid" (Mark 5:2, 3, 4, 15). Serious thought about possessions must start with the capacity of the human body to express the human spirit, to be the medium of human meaning in the world, to be enfleshed word, and, at the same time, with the possibility for this message to be distorted or misread.

Not all the language spoken by our bodies is of universal or immediate intelligibility. The gestures of the body, like the words of a language, exist within the context of a cultural symbolic structure. The same wave of the hand that signals "goodbye" in the United States is, in Guatemala, the sign for "come here." Some biblical "body language" (the tearing of garments, the tossing of dust on the head) is probably rooted in ancient apotropaic gesturing and does not reflect universal responses. The analysis of body language is nevertheless of considerable help in reminding us that, with whatever cultural and historical variations, our bodies *do* express our internal emotions and attitudes. The more elemental the emotion involved, the more likely it is that the corresponding body gesture will have general intelligibility, especially when the emotion is rooted in biological reaction. Our bodies instinctively and involuntarily recoil from danger, crouch in fear, flinch from pain. The surge of adrenalin resulting from fear and anger can cause our bodies to tighten, clench, and even shake. Societal norms channel and camouflage these reactions, it is true, and part of the fascination of body language analysis is in discerning the ways our bodies can learn to express unacceptable emotions in socially acceptable ways. Even given this, some gestures retain altogether incredible longevity: the upraised finger has had a long career as a sign of contempt. I have found it in Dio Chrysostom, and saw it recently while driving through a traffic jam. In the remarks that follow, the symbolizations attached to bodily gestures are those of our Western culture. No pretense is made here of anything other than illustration.

Because we are soul and body, or somatic spirits with an inner and outer life, we are living symbols of ourselves. Our bodies can at times express, even unwillingly, what speech cannot or dares not. In spite of all my casual banter, my rigidly crossed arms before my chest suggest another locution: "I am afraid of you." No matter how smooth and kind my speech, my tightly clenched teeth are saying "I am angry at you." And however much I may speak about generosity and helping another, my closed fist suggests that "I am not letting go, and you will have to fight to get this."

Our bodies are symbols because they reveal, make manifest, our inner emotional states and attitudes. A symbol, however, is more than a sign, even a natural one. Smoke tells us there is fire, but smoke does not burn things up. The body is a symbol in the way a sacrament is a symbol. It is, to borrow the old scholastic definition, a sign that effects what it signifies. The body not only signals the state of my heart, it makes it real in the world outside my mind. Here, too, the traffic moves both ways. Our bodies speak to our minds as much as our minds to our bodies. When I close myself in a tight knot, my body not only expresses fear and defensiveness but strengthens it. We all know that scratching makes an itch real in a way that it wasn't before.

Because the traffic moves both ways, because my body speaks to my spirit, it is possible for me to place my body in witness to my convictions. It is one thing for me to think or say I believe in the resurrection of the dead; it is another to place my body on the line for this conviction. When

I undergo martyrdom for this belief, I testify to others, yes, but first of all to myself, that I believe in the resurrection life. When I remain celibate for the sake of the kingdom, I testify to myself first of all that my longing for life and continued life is not to be found in progeny but in the gift of resurrection. The disposition of my body not only expresses my conviction, it also strengthens that conviction and makes it real.

Our bodies make our attitudes actual most of all because we are social creatures, and our bodies speak within a language of social gestures. Facing each other's bodies, the signs and symbolic exchanges intensify and multiply and become mutually influential. It is one thing to adopt the fetal position when I fall asleep in my own bed; it has quite another impact when I slip into it in the middle of a party. I smile at my neighbor; my body expresses my open and friendly attitude toward the other, and in turn evokes from the other a corresponding smile. It is an effective sign. In other contexts, the same rictus in the middle of my face (this smile) can have quite another meaning and evoke quite another response. A smile can be sardonic and evoke worry; cynical and evoke shame; sadistic and evoke terror. An embrace communicates warmth and acceptance and evokes a responsive embrace. With a bit more pressure and a bit more force, what looks like an embrace can also be a seizure and can evoke a struggle for freedom. Unless the context is clear, the language of the body can be frighteningly ambiguous. Kissing another is probably as universal a symbol of affection as we know; but this, too, can be distorted, as we know from the kiss of Judas in the garden.

Looking at the language of bodily expression, then, we are led to two rather simple conclusions. The first is that our bodies do, inevitably, symbolize something of our inner attitudes, emotional states, and orientation. The second conclusion is that the precise shape of the symbolization is conditioned by a wider context of social symbols — that even the "natural" language of the body speaks without ambiguity only within a clear system of symbolic understanding.

The Symbolic World of Possessions

A question should be occurring to the reader by now. What does all this talk about the symbolism of bodies and the enfleshment of the word in the world by the body have to do with possessions? It has just about everything to do with possessions, in fact. It is in the ambiguity of our somatic/spiritual existence as humans that we properly locate the mystery of human possessions. It is therefore important for us to attend to the shape of the ambiguity we experience regarding our own bodies, these bodies by which we move out into the world outside our minds. Notice that I say "our bodies." I make at once a statement of possession. Isn't this strange? Yet we speak this way all the time. We say, "my hand," "my foot," "my heart." And we recognize that there is truth to this. It is, nevertheless, a veiled and partial truth. When we think about it, we see that we don't *have* bodies in the same way that we *have,* for example, loose change in our pocket.

When I think about it, that is to say, when I furrow the brow, tap the foot, stare off into space, juggle phantasms somewhere in the recesses of the cortex, I conclude that I do not just have a body, but *am* a body. What I know about myself (and other people) involves, totally and without exception, knowing about my body. I do not know what will happen to me when I die; I do not know how I began. But from the first time I remember *me,* I remember my body; and although this increasingly corpulent and increasingly decrepit self has gone through multiple and unflattering changes, it remains the one, constant touchstone of myself, my *self,* me. I know that I will die, and can verify that by logic, if not desire. But although I have observed the death of others and noticed that a "body" remains, it is not a body but a corpse; and, just as I don't know where the soul went, neither do I know where the "body" went, or where "they" went. In the strictest sense, I cannot even imagine (phantasms being concrete and somatic) my own existence apart from this bodily me. I am, irreducibly and convincingly, a body.

Yet, because of this "otherness" to me, this mysterious inner awareness and reflectiveness, by which I not only perceive but am aware of my perception, I can regard even my body as something which I *have,* as a possession. I say "my body," not "my body's me." I can say "the soul's body" or "*my* soul's body." I can even regard this somatic aspect of my self as a "thing" of which I can dispose in various ways. It should be emphasized, I think, that this is no less valid a perception than that which tells me I am a body. There is a built-in ambiguity to our spiritual/somatic existence, which is rooted in our being incarnate: we both are and have bodies. It would be a mistake to think that this is an ambiguity from which we can flee, or one with which we can ever dispense. So long as we remain "in" the body, that is, so long as we remain living human beings, we shall be in this state of tension. The body expresses who I am, and the

body is who I am. I am a living symbol. I am also, inevitably, a *possessor.*
Any thinking about possessions that does not recognize the irreducible
nature of human possessing is fantasy.

But there are degrees of being and having, even within our individual
somatic existence. I can only, in these remarks, appeal to your own experience of things and ask you to judge whether you see them the same
way. I know that I "have" a hand in a truer sense than I "am" a hand. However, I "am" head and heart more than I "have" head and heart. In danger,
I throw up my hand to protect my head rather than the other way
around. I do not impale my heart on a stick to save my hand. I face ampu-
tation of a finger (however sorrowfully) with greater serenity than I contemplate decapitation or disembowelment. Eczema is neither the trag-
edy nor threat to my being that brain cancer is. All of our language about
spiritual activity (that is, the activity of "being") connotes inwardness,
interiority, whether with reference to a specific organ, such as the brain
or heart, or with diffuse imagery. We say "I have a feeling in my bones,"
"It's just a gut feeling." We do not say "It's just an epidural feeling" or "The
fingernail has its ways." We have, I think, a sense of moving *outward* from
being into having. Even with our bodies, our more outward parts are regarded as the more disposable, the more inward parts as the more indis-
pensable. Mental derangement and emotional crippling are regarded by
all of us as threats to the very *being* of a person in a way that the loss of
hair or the crippling of a leg are not.

Material possessions must be seen as lying within this continuum of
being and having, which is an essential aspect of human somatic existence. At the most elementary and popular level, this truth is glimpsed.
We regard tools as the extensions of our bodies. We say that clothes
make the man, the style is the person, you are what you eat. We perceive
that our possessions, the things we have and use, extend our bodies and
our *selves* into the world and into the lives of other persons. What we
wear, eat, dwell in, drive, and use all express who we are and what we are.
Possessions are symbolic expressions of ourselves because we both are
and have bodies. Every claim of ownership, therefore, involves an ambiguity; we say, this is *mine,* but we imply as well, this is *me.* Our possessions extend not only our bodies as possessions into the world but also
our bodies as our *selves.* In every act of ownership, therefore, is a claim to
being as well.

Just as the way we dispose of our bodies expresses and affects our inner disposition, so our self-disposition expresses and affects our disposi-

tion of possessions. When I throw my *body* between you and the exit, I am making a statement of power: you must either go through, over, or around me to get to the door. When I throw up a *wall* around my property, I am making precisely the same statement. When I shake *my fist* in your face, I am making a statement of anger and aggression; when I shake a *stick,* or an *arrest warrant* in your face, I am making precisely the same statement. When I open wide my *arms* to greet you, I am stating a welcome; when I open wide the *doors* of my house as you walk by, I am making precisely the same statement. The disposition of possessions symbolizes our self-disposition in the same way that our bodies symbolize our selves.

The way we use, own, acquire, and disperse material things symbolizes and expresses our attitudes and responses to our selves, the world around us, other people, and, most of all, God. And since there is reciprocity here, as well, the disposition of material possessions not only expresses but *affects* our response to the world, other people, and God. Just as there is an inherent ambiguity to being and having a body, so there is inevitably ambiguity in the employment of material possessions. The real difficulty regarding possessions lies in what they mean to us. The real mystery concerning possessions is how they relate to our sense of identity and worth as human beings. The real sin related to possessions has to do with the willful confusion of being and having.

It is necessary to make clear here that it is simply not a question of how much or how little possession is involved. Quantitative considerations are secondary, not primary. Certainly, for human life to continue at all, a certain amount of food, a certain amount of clothing, and a certain adequacy of shelter from the elements is necessary. But even at the level of subsistence, the question of meaning is critical. We have heard from survivors of concentration camps how, even in the midst of general starvation and the leveling effect of complete servitude, a single slice of moldy bread or cup of watery soup could and did serve a symbolic function. For this individual, stealing a slice of bread meant a grasping of power; by taking from another's ration, he could survive another day. For another, giving away her ration of bread meant certain death but symbolized her willingness to die that another might live. We also know how, in a home for the aged, a rocking chair in a sunny window can become a bone of bitter contention and lead even to murder. A young monk once cleaned out the cell of an exemplary and virtuous monk who had died. He found in a trunk under the bed cartons and cartons of Lucky Strike

Greens, cigarettes hoarded away since before the Second World War and never smoked but just stored for thirty years in a lonely cell in a remote monastery.

Physical deprivation, or destitution, does not by itself either ennoble or degrade human beings; but it is terribly effective at revealing the fundamental issues. For all of us, possessions are not simply "out there" as neutral objects. They are also "in here," wrapped up in our sense of who we are and what we are worth. The issue of meaning is determinative.

We recognize, simply on the human level, that there is a serious derangement when a man throws his body into a raging fire to rescue his television set, or when a mother leaves a baby alone in a cold apartment in order to go out shopping for a new dress. We suspect the same sort of displacement when a man is willing to destroy his family for career advancement. We sense that something has gone seriously awry in these people's understanding of themselves and the world, that they have a profound confusion in their grasp of being and having. We may recognize as well that there is a greater internal resemblance than at first may appear between an entrepreneur who will go to any lengths to gain a monopoly and the teenager who will go to any lengths to win at Monopoly.

The symbolic meaning of possessions, of owning and having, is very much determined by the fundamental perceptions of the nature of human existence in the world and the origin and goal of the human project. These perceptions, of course, are not determined afresh by every individual, but are shaped to a large extent by the culture or society that presents to individuals a symbolic world for them to accept and use as the framework for their individual perceptions. In a cultural setting as diffuse, pluralistic, and rapidly changing as that in contemporary America, the meanings are constantly in flux. Taking candy away from a baby used to signify meanness. In some sugarphobic circles today it would be regarded as an act of highest virtue. Why there has been this change in significance to the same action is a fascinating question, but it has something to do with a notion of "health" as an absolute and unquestioned value within this culture. The issues of what possessions and body language mean change within the shifting of these basic orientations. One would be hard pressed, for example, to distinguish *physically* between what happens when rowing a slave galley and when working out on a conditioning machine as part of a football team, but the *symbolic* resonances are distinctly different.

The values attached by a society, or subgroup of shared perception within a society, to bodily expression and the disposition of possessions emerge in turn from an overarching theological anthropology. This is an understanding, frequently incoherent and implicit, to be sure, of what it means to be a worthwhile human being in the world and where the ultimate source of that worth is to be found. The frantic efforts of slick magazines to put the "right stuff" (as Tom Wolfe had it) before their readers makes sense only if having the "right stuff" means, within this society, being the "right kind of person." Whatever the ecological variations (what is rare here being common there, and its value being affected thereby), the meaning attached to possessions as such corresponds to the measure of human worth. This is the case even when the measure of the dominant culture is rejected. The rough cloak and staff of the ancient cynic philosopher or the deviant dress of whatever passes for a counterculture in contemporary America (however the deviant dress is defined; one cannot keep up with this) have this in common: possessions are not, and cannot be, eliminated, but take on a different symbolic value.

The Symbolic Function of Possessions in Scripture

It is at this point in our thinking about possessions that we can return to the Scriptures. My remarks on the human mystery of possessing have only touched on the issues, but they have at least, perhaps, alerted us to the sort of questions we should put to Scripture, or allow it to put to us. Unless we have tried to reflect in a concrete and creative way on what something means in our actual lives — whether we are talking about possessions or power or sexuality or whatever — and until we begin to get a sense that we are talking about something real — not an abstract problem, but a fundamental aspect of the mystery of human existence in the world, that is, human existence before God — we are not yet ready to hear God's Word addressed to our actual lives.

The writings of the Old and New Testaments are not simply about the history of Israel, the ministry of Jesus, and the beginnings of the church, though such a history can be derived from those writings. What the Scriptures are *about*, first of all, is the gift and goal of human existence as it has been called into being by the one God who reveals himself in the world and in the history of his creatures. This is the one God who calls the world into being at every moment, and calls into faith his people in every age; and because he is the one God who is ever present and ever the same, before whom time and space, like all contingent categories, fade, we are contemporary with those to whom the words first came. The Word of God in Scripture as it speaks to the mystery of human existence in the world speaks as directly to us as it did to them.

Idolatry and Possessions

I have been suggesting that the importance of possessions, above all, lies in what they mean to the one claiming possession and the way they symbolize the human response to reality. It is to this expressive, symbolic function of possessions that the Word of God most directly speaks. And, as the symbolism of owning and having is intelligible only within a wider framework of symbolic understanding, so is this the case with the Christian understanding of possessions. There is a theological anthropology presumed by Christian existence and reflection — a perception of the meaning of human existence in the world and with other persons, which emerges from the fundamental fact and challenge of that existence as enunciated by God's Word: faith in the one creating, sustaining, and saving God, blessed forever. It is within the understanding of reality established by faith in God that the Christian use of possessions finds its meaning. It is to the nature of that faith, and the understanding of humanity, world, and God that it presumes, that we must now attend.

The fundamental human response is not, first, to what is seen, but to the one who is unseen (Heb. 11:3). The way a person responds to God determines all other responses to the world and to other persons in the world, for God is what is most real. If the response to ultimate reality, the one who is most real and therefore most true, is missed and distorted, then all other responses become distorted as well. This is the issue posed by monotheistic faith: to choose between reality and illusion, truth and falsehood. The choice made here is of the most far-reaching consequence, for if the truth about point of origin and destination of the world and humans is not grasped accurately, then the significance of the world and of humans within it is also perverted. The choice put before human freedom at every moment in every age is this: to acknowledge as ultimate and determinative either that power which is implicit and unseen or those powers within the world which are explicit and all too palpable. The conflict for monotheism is between faith in the one God and idolatry.

On Sinai the Word came to Israel, "I am the Lord your God, who brought you out of the land of Egypt, out of the house of bondage. You shall have no other gods before me. You shall not make for yourself a graven image, or any likeness of anything that is in the heaven above, or that is in the earth beneath, or that is in the water under the earth; you shall not bow down to them and serve them" (Exod. 20:2-5). The confession of Israel in response to this call is: "Hear, O Israel: The Lord our God is one Lord; and you shall love the Lord your God with all your heart, and with all your soul, and with all your might" (Deut. 6:4-5).

This confession of Yahweh as the one God, it need not be stressed, is not a matter of intellectual affirmation or assent to a proposition. That kind of "faith" was called "dead" by the writer James, who said, "You believe that God is one; you do well. Even the demons believe — and shudder" (James 2:19). No, this faith is a kind of obediential hearing; it is a matter of acknowledging a claim made upon human existence by the one who called that existence into being; a matter of trust that such an acknowledgment will not go astray; a matter of service; a matter of directing human freedom in response to the one who established that freedom. The passage in Deuteronomy continues, "You shall fear the Lord your God; you shall serve him, and swear by his name. You shall not go after other gods, of the gods of the peoples who are round about you; for the Lord your God in the midst of you is a jealous God" (Deut. 6:13-15).

That there is but one ultimate power to be reckoned with is as central to the Christian confession as to the Jewish. The "Hear, O Israel" is found on the lips of Jesus (Mark 12:29; cf. Matt. 22:37; Luke 10:27), and the oneness of God is everywhere the presupposition of faith in Jesus as his Son (see Rom. 3:30; 10:12; 1 Cor. 8:4-6; 2 Cor. 4:5-6; 1 Thess. 1:9; 1 Tim. 2:5; Heb. 6:1; James 1:17-18; 1 Pet. 1:17). The confession of Jesus as Lord forced Christians to a new understanding of God's unity, it is true, but for Christians as well as Jews, Abraham remains the father of faith in the one God, even though the Christian articulation of the faith adds, "him that raised from the dead Jesus our Lord" (Rom. 4:24; cf. Rom. 10:9).

The prophets of Yahweh who railed against the oppression of the needy within Israel (to which we will return in the next chapter) saw such oppression as a consequence of idolatry. For the prophets, as for the Deuteronomic historians and for the Apostle Paul, the battle in the human heart is as always one waged between trust in the true God and trust in idols. If we are to get any further in our reflection, we must decide whether or not what they are talking about makes any sense for us. Is this business of idolatry a matter of ancient political and tribal rivalries writ large in cosmic powers, or does it really involve genuine and enduring issues for human freedom? We must cut through the mockery of some prophetic descriptions of idolatry, and the sarcasm of some of the Wisdom writers, to see idolatry as it is, not a droll but harmless quirk of ancient peoples but an endemic disease of the human spirit. Idolatry as a theological category points to a fundamental perversion of human freedom. It is, if anything is, a contemporary issue. It deserves some attention.

There are two places in the Scriptures where the writer tries to do more than dismiss idolatry as sheer nonsense: in the Wisdom of Solomon and in Paul's letter to the Romans. Both Paul and the Wisdom writer try to get inside this phenomenon, to understand (as far as a Jew could) how humans could so miss the mark. The Wisdom writer is by far the gentler of the two. He supposes that the minds of idolaters have been seduced by the beauty of creation and that, although the shape of the world should have led them to the knowledge of the Creator (13:5), still, the folly of idolaters (13:1) is at least understandable: "They trust in what they see, because the things that are seen are beautiful" (13:7). Nevertheless, the idolater is one to be pitied: "Miserable, with hopes set on dead things, are the men who give the name 'gods' to the works of men's hands, gold and silver fashioned with skill" (13:10). We see here that idolatry involves the misplacement of hope and trust. This cuts to the heart of the matter. The one who trusts in what is not the ultimate source of power needs to support the object of his or her trust (13:16). Idols only exist, in other words, in virtue of service. Since whatever is not God is contingent, that is, not the necessary or sufficient cause of its own existence, it cannot give life but can only receive it. The promise of life held out by idols, therefore, is deceptive; they become "traps for the souls of men and as snares to the feet of the foolish" (14:11). Since idols are but the projections of human desires (13:17-19), they reflect the bondage of human freedom (14:21). The folly of idolatry lies in seeking life where it cannot be found, in the works of human hands. Indeed, human beings have more life than their idols: "he is mortal, and what he makes with lawless hands is dead. For he is better than the objects he worships, since he has life, but they never have" (15:17).

The author of the Wisdom of Solomon sees idolatry, therefore, as a fundamental error about the world and its source, an error that is not simply intellectual but also religious. Idolatry is "the beginning and cause and end of every evil" (14:27), for it leads, in addition to all forms of corruption and human hostility, to "confusion over what is good" (14:25-26). The fundamental error about God, he suggests, leads to an inability even to perceive what is good in the world. By seeking health, riches, power, and security from the powers that were supposed to reside behind them, these idolaters "thought wickedly of God" (14:30). If those who worship idols are to be pitied, the one who encourages such worship by making idols for profit is one who truly sins, "because he failed to know the One who formed him and inspired him with an active soul and breathed into him a living spirit. But he considered our existence an idle game, and life a festival held for profit, for he says one must get money however one can, even by base means. For this man, more than all others, knows that he sins when he makes from earthy matter fragile vessels and graven images" (15:11-13). Two points can be made quickly on this last citation from the Wisdom of Solomon. Notice, first, that the "knowledge" of God does not come only, or even especially, from some argument from nature, but from personal existential experience: all the man needed to do was listen to his own breathing. Second, notice that we have here, not at all for the first or last time, the explicit connection of idolatry and covetousness.

If the sympathy of the Wisdom writer for idolaters is minimal, that of Paul in Romans is nonexistent. He states emphatically that idolaters are "without excuse" (Rom. 1:20). Paul agrees with the Wisdom writer that God's power and deity can be discerned from the things that have been made (1:20), but whereas the Wisdom writer attributed idolatry to the seductive beauty of creation, Paul asserts that it derives from a choice not to acknowledge the claim of the Creator upon his creatures: "although they knew God they did not honor him as God or give thanks to him" (1:21). Thus, for Paul, idolatry is the "big lie"; it is the suppression of the truth (1:18) about human existence in the world. It is a willful refusal to acknowledge reality. From this fundamental rebellion, this refusal to acknowledge the truth even after it has been perceived, there results a distorted view of the rest of reality; creation itself gets skewed in the eyes of the idolater. The big lie spawns many smaller ones. Paul sees the perverted relations between men and women, the hostile attitudes and actions of people toward each other, as stemming from this basic darkening of the mind (1:21) that comes about when people refuse to allow God to make a claim upon their existence: "they exchanged the truth about God for a lie and worshiped and served the creature rather than the Creator, who is blessed forever! Amen" (Rom. 1:25). Paul speaks of

God progressively "handing them over" (1:24, 26, 28) to their misconceptions, perverse attitudes, and behavior; and he calls the judgment coming upon them the revelation of "God's wrath" (1:18). But it is clear that this alienation from God, with its resulting alienation from the self and other humans, is a result of human freedom; it comes about because of disobedience, a rejection at the most profound level, of the truth about one's own being in the world as not sufficient unto itself but coming from God. Therefore, Paul says that the results of this distortion and disobedience work themselves out precisely in the way those perceptions lead to ever more ruinous conflict and deadly competition: "receiving in their own persons the due penalty for their error" (1:27). For both the Wisdom writer and Paul, therefore, the issue of idolatry is not one of casual alternative forms of piety. It is a disease of freedom by which people get enslaved, and a sickness of intelligence by which minds are darkened. From the choice of idolatry stems the distortion of reality and relations between people in the world.

It is important at this point to return to our own experience. Just as we could not grasp anything significant about possessions before we looked at the way our bodies operate in owning, so these words of Scripture on idolatry will float abstractly above us, unless we make an attempt to locate the issue they address in the fabric of our own lives. Let us, then, take idolatry as a functional category and try to see how it works in human life.

Idolatry, in simple terms, is the choice of treating as ultimate and absolute that which is neither absolute nor ultimate. We treat something as ultimate by the worship we pay it — meaning here, of course, neither the worship of lips nor of incense but of service. Worship is service. Functionally, then, my god is that which I serve by my freedom. Whatever I may claim as ultimate, the truth is that my god is that which rivets my attention, centers my activity, preoccupies my mind, and motivates my action. That in virtue of which I act is god; that for which I will give up anything else is my god. Diagnostically, I can tell what my god is by seeing what it is around which the patterns of my life organize themselves.

Our lives, after all, do form patterns. Our freedom is not found in scattered outbursts of random activity, but in the shaping of a direction. There is in all our lives some sort of consistency in response to situations. We do not do this one moment, and the opposite the next moment, totally at random. Even if it is hard to discern, even if erratic or eccentric, there is a pattern to our lives that manifests itself in the many small responses we make moment by moment, day by day. The patterns in our lives form around the deep and usually unarticulated attitudes we hold toward ourselves, the world, and others. Within this fundamental orientation of our lives, our personal project of existence is being formed. The choices we make at this or that moment flow out of this orientation and either strengthen or weaken it.

It is not hard to see how this is the case for someone who has a deeply rooted fear of others, perhaps even a form of paranoia. The perception that others are against me, that others are out to get me, that everyone is concerned about me all the time structures the ways I respond to others (distrustfully, defensively, suspiciously), and if things run true to form, I will emerge from each encounter with my suspicions verified and my orientation of fear and distrust deepened. In sharp contrast is the pattern of one who is able to trust, who views the world and other people positively. The choices made by such an individual tend to flow from that trusting attitude, and these choices tend to be confirmed by the trust received in return.

Phenomenologists of religion have been telling us for some time that the human creature is one that inevitably *centers* itself in this world, and does so by choice. The primordial sense of creatureliness, that is, our accurate perception that we are powerless and without self-generated worth, moves the human creature to seek power and worth in something outside the self. The human organism is instinctually impoverished and existentially threatened; meaning does not come to us automatically or easily. We do not have a place in the world given simply by birth and instinct as do cats and dogs. Somehow, it is the centering activity of our freedom that we seek this place in the world and our significance. Where the center is located determines the pattern of human activity. The behavioral significance of sacred times and spaces lies in this: around the place where the holy (the powerful) appears, human activity finds its organizational principle. It is from the center that the human person expects power, meaning, identity, worth — everything, in short, that should go with *being*.

We are the lonely creatures, then, who find ourselves lacking worth and meaning (we are not the sufficient cause of our own being) and who feel impelled to seek them outside ourselves. Where we identify the source of our life and power (our *being*) and our worth is for us our center, and our center organizes the patterns of our perceptions from which our actions flow. Where the center is, there is our god.

LIBRARY, UNIVERSITY OF CHESTER

One might legitimately ask here whether this is too simple a picture of the way we deploy our freedom, and in a sense it is. I am not suggesting that the patterns of which I speak are locked irrevocably and clearly around some specific center. What I am suggesting is that the truest use of our freedom is not found in the choice of this thing or that, this action or that, but in the *direction* of those individual choices, and this direction involves centering. Nor am I suggesting that a pattern, once established, cannot be broken or changed; quite the contrary, we are always, so long as we are alive, in the process of shaping our direction, our fundamental attitude. Specific choices are not thereby demeaned; they become more significant than ever. It is true that the way we perform in any given situation tends to arise out of our fundamental perceptions and attitudes, but what happens in that choice also tends to strengthen or weaken the fundamental stance we are adopting toward reality. A small opening in trust may enable another slightly larger opening, and if that is received, then another, so that my orientation toward life, with each small response, can become fundamentally more open and trusting. The same is true, of course, of the opposite pattern: a small choice of closure, of selfishness or distrust, can begin the erosion of an attitude toward life that was fundamentally trusting. We can see the truth of this in the dynamics of human relationships. Love between people is seldom ruptured unless there is much erosion before. And the erosion is accomplished precisely by the small, then larger, then massive incidents of distrust and misunderstanding, which build up until there is a wall between us where before there had been intimacy and freedom.

The test of whether we do in fact center our freedom this way is not whether or not anthropologists say the Trobriand Islanders do it, but whether it happens in our lives. It is necessary for us, if the category of idolatry is to mean something, to look at the shape of our own lives. There are patterns to be discerned in the flow of our days, months, and years, in the movement of our days, in the shaping of our relationships. Much of our time, it is true, is spent in routine work and maintenance. But if we look carefully, we can see that there are organizing principles around which the ordinary revolves — the high points, the turning points, whether of anticipation or dread, that structure our day.

Some questions like the following may help us get the point: What is it, really, that enables us to get up and face each day's activity? What is it that we will make room for during the day, no matter how busy our schedule? By what measure do I look back over the day, or week, or year, and consider it a success or a failure? In the daily round, is the high point the end of work and the beginning of leisure? The first drink? Is that which I will fit into my schedule no matter what my three-mile jog? When I lie awake in my bed with a feeling of discontent, is it because I did not get done all the work I intended to do that day, or did not get some time to myself, or did not spend time with my children and wife, or looked foolish in a conference, or dread facing a job interview tomorrow? When I look at others of my own generation, as I suspect we all do, and think about "where I am" in my life, what measurement do I use? Do I think of myself as a success or failure in relation to others, and on what basis — my health, my wealth, my work (process or product), my fame, my family, my power over others, my good looks? These are not complicated questions, but they are, for most of us, difficult ones, for they have a way, cumulatively, of locating our center. And this brings us back, somewhat circuitously, to idolatry. For, if idolatry is a functional phenomenon, the real question comes when I ask, "Where is it that the meaning and power of my individual human life is sought? In what or where do I seek my sense of worth and identity? What is it, seen or unseen, which is the 'bottom line' for me, the source of my hope? What is it without which life would not be worth living? What is it for which I move and act, without which I stumble and fall? What gets me depressed? What is it, in my actual life, that functions as my god?"

Counterfeits are the more dangerous the closer they come to the genuine article. No one is much hurt by a wooden nickel, for no one is much fooled by it. But people can be badly hurt by artfully printed thousand-dollar bills, for they work, and work big, and yet are nothing but illusion. The important idolatries have always centered on those forces that have enough specious power to be truly counterfeit, and therefore truly dangerous: sexuality (fertility), riches, and power (or glory).

The attractiveness of idolatry lies in its claim to manipulate ultimate power; the folly of idolatry lies in the fact that any power that can be manipulated cannot be ultimate. The idolater says, "This which I can see and feel and handle and use, which is within my disposition, is the ultimate source of my worth, my identity, my security, my being. The power I *have* is the measurement of my value." For idolatry, Feuerbach is certainly correct — these gods are but the projection of primitive human needs. For the true God, Feuerbach is absolutely wrong. Idolaters are persons who, filled with the terror of nonbeing and worthlessness — the built-in threat of contingency — must construct their own worth (as the Scriptures have it) "with the works of their own hands."

When we hand over the measurement of ourselves to forces that are just as much created as we are, then our gods are truly illusory. And if that which we acknowledge as ultimate can only remain so in virtue of our service, can only be ultimate because of our choice of it as such, then we are indeed fools. This illusion and folly is completely compatible, we should note, with a verbal confession of the "true god"; idolatry flourishes as much within orthodoxy as without. We can pledge allegiance to the most orthodox and theologically discriminating of creeds; it does not matter. Idolatry is found in the service of the heart, the way we concretely and existentially dispose of our freedom: "This people honors me with their lips, but their heart is far from me; in vain do they worship me . . ." (Mark 7:6-7; Isa. 29:13 LXX).

The truly depressing thing about idolatry is that, by making the relative absolute, the contingent necessary, and the end-all that which is neither end nor all, we have distorted reality — not just the "reality" outside us, but the whole orientation of ourselves in the world. Not only do we close ourselves off from the true source of our being and worth; we also close ourselves off from that very thing we worship. We no longer see it as it is, and therefore we worship not the thing itself, but our desire for it to be god. A creature perceived as god cannot but be diminished by that perception. Not only that, but the being and freedom we seek are also diminished, for in feeding our idol our own sustenance is drained. Seeking freedom, we end in enslavement, for no worldly power can establish us in freedom, but only bind us when we worship it. All idolatry is a form of compulsion. We must compulsively labor, must endlessly toil to strengthen this god that has no existence beyond that which we give it.

Another consequence of this idolatrous structuring of our lives is that we are closed off from the rest of the world, too, once we establish one part of the world as divine. One who lives solely and ultimately for pleasure finds little joy in work and, for that matter, little in pleasure. Total dedication to making money has had documented disastrous effects on sexual activity. Ruthless ambition for power over others leaves one with few friends. The great dictators and petty hedonists alike are dismal figures to contemplate: Hitler falling asleep at his own conversation; Dorian Gray with one eye on his portrait; Howard Hughes watching old movies in the dark while his fingernails grow.

Centering our hope in what we can grasp leads to the loss not only of the richness of creation as a whole, but even of that we thought we had hold of. As Qoheleth ("the Preacher") tartly remarked, "He who loves money will not be satisfied with money; nor he who loves wealth, with gain: this also is vanity" (Eccles. 5:10). An idolater seeks life where it cannot be found, but the idolater, like every other human being, must die, and with death the idol must die as well. "Again, I saw vanity under the sun: a person who has no one, either son or brother, yet there is no end to all his toil, and his eyes are never satisfied with riches, so that he never asks, 'For whom am I toiling and depriving myself of pleasure?' This also is vanity and an unhappy business" (Eccles. 4:7-8). The compulsive toil expended in establishing our worth in what we can handle and point to is wasted: "just as he came, so shall he go; and what gain has he that he toiled for the wind, and spent all his days in darkness and grief, in much vexation and sickness and resentment?" (Eccles. 5:16-17).

Idolatry is self-alienation. The self is sought where it cannot be found, in the possession of another creature. Deep within us gnaws the dread of nonbeing and worthlessness. This is a proper self-recognition for a creature. But the move of idolatry is to refuse the truth that our being and worth come to us from another, the one who created us. If we do not have being ourselves, and if we refuse to acknowledge the dependence of our existence on another, then we must work ceaselessly to create ourselves out of the things around us. We must toil to create a "being" and a "worth" in this world — what we have, what we use, whom we can manipulate, dominate, stroke. And then we will be able to say, "There I am." This is a sad charade. It is, as Qoheleth said, vanity.

I spoke of riches as being one of the classic objects of idolatry. When we look at the matter more closely, however, we see that every form of idolatry is a form of possessiveness. Whether it be beauty, material things, power, or prestige, the centering of ourselves on some created reality as ultimate involves a claim of possessing. This which I have is the touchstone of my worth, the supporter of my identity and being. An idolater is one who, quite literally, seeks to have god in his pocket. The power worshiped is shown service precisely so that it can be controlled. The idolater seeks to *own* god, and since the true God cannot be owned, the idolater fashions one more amenable to manipulation. By possessing what we identify as our ultimate power, we make claim to possessing ourselves. In this light, we may be able better to appreciate the puzzling shorthand of Colossians 3:5, "covetousness, which is idolatry," or that of Ephesians 5:5: "Be sure of this, that no immoral or impure man, or one who is covetous (that is, an idolater), has any inheritance in the kingdom of Christ and of God." All idolatry is a form of covetousness, for by refusing to acknowledge life and worth as a gift from the Creator, it seeks to seize them from the creation as booty. Enough on this sickness; let us turn to the light.

Faith and Possessions

God is what is most real. This is the starting point of the believer. God is not that which is "left over" when all else has been accounted for, or a thing among other things; nor is God locked into an infinite chain of contingent causality. God is the Cause that underlies all causing, the power of being who calls into being, the infinite horizon against which the world we perceive is measured. These affirmations, it need not be said, do not stem from the findings of science but from the stance of faith. The believer's perception of the human condition begins, just as the idolater's, with the pain, fear, fragility, and transitoriness of human life (Pss. 90:3-10; 102:23-24; 103:14-16; 144:4). Belief in the true God does not alter the structure of human existence, does not relieve us of contingency; but it does transform the meaning of our existence. The idolater says, "I am alone in the world and must seek to establish myself to have life." The believer says, "I have been established in real but partial being in the world by another, and must seek him as the giver of my life." The believer, as aware of the perilousness of human life as the idolater, refuses to flee from this contingency, but embraces it by acknowledging that what partial life he or she has comes from the Creator and Sustainer of life, and that to seek further life elsewhere is illusory. The Promethean impulse is rejected. Yahweh God is not simply another cosmic force available for manipulation. God is the inaccessible (yet surprisingly encountered) power behind and within all that exists, and refuses to be captured by name or definition. He is not just a tribal deity, or the projection of human desires; God is the one who fashions all that exists, here and now, by his Word (Pss. 24:1-2; 33:6-9; 47:7; 50:9-12; 65:5-8; 95:4-6; 100:3; 102:25-27; 104:1ff.; 119:90; 121:2; 124:8; 136:5-9; 148:5-6). He is the one who, here and now, gives life (existence) to all creatures (Pss. 81:10; 104:27-30; 107:9, 33-38; 111:5; 119:73; 136:25; 145:15). If God is the ultimate source of all that is, the immediate cause of every breath taken by human beings (1 Sam. 2:6) — and there is no serious talk about God unless this is where we begin — then before

God every created power is relative and derivative. Whatever power is claimed for idols is literally as nothing compared to the power of God (Pss. 81:9-10; 86:8; 89:6-13; 96:5-6; 97:7-9; 115:3-7; 135:5-7, 15-18), for whatever natural or human force lies behind the idol itself comes from God.

It should be recognized that this is not a matter of logical reckoning, but of the acknowledgment of reality. We do not need to decipher the universe to make this acknowledgment, but only place our fingers at the vein in our temple and ponder the thin wall of flesh that separates us from darkness. We need only draw a breath, and then ask, how can I do this? Of course, I can also look at the fragility and "nonnecessity" of my being and refuse to acknowledge my dependence on God. That is why there can be no convincing proof of God's existence for those who do not wish to make this recognition, no argument that will be compelling. In this matter, we have all made our choices already. The believer can support the option of faith with towering metaphysical arguments, but these are not what led him or her to faith. If idolatry, as Paul suggests, is a refusal to acknowledge and honor God as God, no less is belief in God as Creator and Sustainer of life a matter of choice: "By faith we understand that the world was created by the word of God, so that what is seen was made out of things which do not appear" (Heb. 11:3).

I have spoken of idolatry as a functional derangement of the human spirit and suggested that one can give intellectual assent to the proposition that there is but one God and still pattern one's life idolatrously. The opposite, I think, is also true. Genuine faith in the one God is available even to those whose intellectual perceptions or religious traditions place them within the category that would ordinarily be called "unbelief." If God is what is most real, he is what is most true, as well. The human response to truth (that is, existential truth, the truth about one's own existence), in however fragmented and partial a form, is an approach to the true God. The person whose attitudes and actions truly acknowledge the claim of truth (God) on his or her existence, and opens himself or herself to that claim in the situations of life, is effectively believing in the one God. To think otherwise is to limit God and make him an idol of our creedal fashioning.

The consequences of existential (that is to say, actual) faith in the creating and sustaining God pervade all our perceptions of and responses to the world. If there is but one ultimate power, and it is not located within creation but is, rather, its presupposition, then all of the world is established in its proper place, as creature. By calling holy only the one who is the ultimate being, we allow all other beings to exist, not as gods (and therefore falsely) but simply as "the world" (and therefore authentically). To acknowledge that my every breath comes from God, that I am sustained out of nothingness (here and now!) only by God's loving care, is to assert my radical dependence upon God and God only. To recognize that my existence is established only by God's gift is to realize as well not only my radical and irreducible poverty but also God's overwhelming gift. (For without life what do I have? Yet I can neither account for, nor add to, this life.) My existence is not something I have or possess. It comes to me, without my having any say about it, from another as a gift. In the strictest sense, I *am* but do not *have* my own existence. I have no sufficient reason, in and of myself, for my being here or continuing here. The statement of Job, "Naked I came from my mother's womb, and naked shall I return; the Lord gave, and the Lord has taken away" (Job 1:21; cf. Eccles. 5:13-16), is true not only for the entry and exit of my life, but for every moment in between as well. As beings created every day from nothing, we stand perpetually naked before the Lord, for not even our breath is our own (see 1 Tim. 6:7).

This leads to a further recognition. Everything else in creation (everything else that is not God) stands before God just the way we do. "The earth is the Lord's and the fulness thereof, the world and all those who dwell therein; for he has founded it upon the seas, and established it upon the rivers" (Ps. 24:1-2; cf. Ps. 95:4-5). Or, as Paul puts it, "although there may be so-called gods in heaven or on earth — as indeed there are many 'gods' and many 'lords' — yet for us there is one God, the Father, from whom are all things and for whom we exist, and one Lord, Jesus Christ, through whom are all things and through whom we exist" (1 Cor. 8:5-6). The world itself stands before God as creature, as radically dependent. If the earth is "his," and we are "his," there is not, in the final analysis, a sense in which we truly possess *anything*. The world is not ours to possess; it belongs to another. Other people are not ours to possess; they belong to another (Rom. 14:4, 8). With the gift of life, he has given us as well the use and enjoyment of the world but not its keeping. What a confusion there is in our hearts when we think that we not only "own" things, but can find in what we own our life and security. If this is so even of our bodies (and here we come to the ultimate ambiguity of our "being" and "having" bodies), which are frail vessels ready to crack open and spill our lives at the slightest tap, how much more is this the case for the grain we pile in barns or the certificates we store in banks?

But if we are radically poor before God, we are also radically gifted. This is the other side to our creatureliness. However differently we must construe the verb "to be" when used of us and when we apply it by analogy to God, it is the possibility of that verb being used of us at all that points to the source of our identity and worth. By giving us "being" (not, of course, a quantity or quality, but simply the act), by establishing us in existence, God has granted us a share in the "life" that only he can truly be said to possess. While we are held in being by God, we are not empty, we are not devoid of significance, for we truly "are." We need not create ourselves anew, for we are being created now in God's image as he sustains us out of nothingness. We need only accept the gift and allow its growth in freedom, which is to say, in thanksgiving.

When we see our lives in this fashion, we are able to see the lives of other people in the same way. They, too, are held out of nothingness only by the gift of God's loving care. At the level of existence, we are all equally poor, and equally rich. There is nothing we can add to our "being," for it all comes from God. And as we do not, in any proper sense, possess anything, neither does any other human being. As creatures, we meet each other at the level of the most radical equality, the only sort worth speaking of — existential equality. Our shared existence is equally precarious and equally secure, for it comes from God. One would not ordinarily turn to the Proverbs for metaphysical statements, but the following verses, I think, can be read that way: "The rich and the poor meet together; the Lord is the maker of them all" (Prov. 22:2), and, in another passage, "The poor man and the oppressor meet together; the Lord gives light to the eyes of both" (Prov. 29:13).

The most significant consequence of faith in the one God is the potential for freedom it grants us. Because the reality is that we are rooted in the ultimate power of existence itself, because our identity and worth come not from what we can claim to possess but in what is given to us at every moment, and because we acknowledge this reality, we are freed from the need to create or support our being by the control of other things. We need not fearfully and compulsively construct some part of creation as our ultimate center and seek our worth in bondage to its service. As servants of the living God, we are free to use material things without being possessed by them. If the logic of idolatry leads to the attempt to grasp life by what can be possessed, the logic of belief in the true God leads to the refusal to identify what can be possessed with life.

The same God who creates us at every moment from nothingness calls us at every moment into relationship with himself; Abraham is called by believers "the father of us all" (Rom. 4:16), for not only is he the first in the biblical story to be called to faith, but his response is paradigmatic for all of us who are so called by the one "who gives life to the dead and calls into existence the things that do not exist" (Rom. 4:17). When God called Abram to "go from your country and your kindred and your father's house to the land that I will show you" (Gen. 12:1), Abram was a wealthy and well-established man (Gen. 12:5). His faith in God was articulated by his obediential hearing. He did not identify his life with his home, his family, or his family's gods, but, on the strength of God's promise, he became a sojourner, a displaced person in an alien and hostile environment. He allowed his identity to be determined by the one who called him and who as yet had shown no fulfillment of his promise.

Abram did not cease being wealthy; indeed, his possessions increased after he was called (Gen. 12:16). In Genesis 13:2, we read, "Abram was very rich in cattle, in silver, and in gold." Abram's nephew Lot was also wealthy, so much so that "the land could not support both of them dwelling together; for their possessions were so great that they could not dwell together," and there was strife between the herdsmen of Abram and those of Lot (Gen. 13:6-7). For Abram, his kinship with Lot was more important than the right to property (13:8), and he gave his nephew first choice of dwelling place in the land; Lot chose the garden valley which "was well watered everywhere like the garden of the Lord" and went there to dwell (Gen. 13:10). As Abram refused to become enriched at the expense of his kinsman, so did he refuse to profit at the expense of the king of Sodom when Abram's men recovered all the goods of that city taken in a raid by the four kings (Gen. 14:1ff.): "I will take nothing but what the young men have eaten, and the share of the men who went with me" (14:24).

Later generations would look to Abraham as the model of hospitality, for he welcomed God in the guise of the three visitors (Gen. 18:1ff.; cf. Heb. 13:2). But the ultimate test of Abraham's faith was the call to sacrifice his son Isaac (Gen. 22:1ff.). Not only was Isaac Abraham's "only son, . . . whom you love" (22:2), he was the means through which God's own promise of the blessing was to be fulfilled (15:5-6; 17:21). More than that, Isaac was not a son "according to the flesh" (that is, according to Abraham's own striving for an heir, that he might grasp the blessing, Gen. 15:2; 16:2-3); he was a son "according to the promise" (Rom. 9:7-8). He was God's own gift of life to Abraham, given when Abraham's own power of generation was as good as dead, and his wife's womb, as well, was "dead" (Rom. 4:19). For Abraham to sacrifice Isaac meant his risking the possession of the promise. It also meant giving back to God his dearest possession, and by so doing, acknowledging that Isaac's life came from God every moment as a gift. His willingness to do so was the highest and purest act of obediential hearing and trust. Abraham was not even giving up his own project; as far as he knew, he was also giving up God's project for him! But Abraham refused to identify himself by his possessions, even that one given him specially by God. "By faith Abraham, when he was tested, offered up Isaac, and he who had received the promises was ready to offer up his only son, of whom it was said, 'Through Isaac shall your descendants be named.' He considered that God was able to raise men even from the dead; hence, figuratively speaking, he did receive him back" (Heb. 11:17-19). Because Abraham could leave even his dearest possession for the sake of life before God, he can be called "friend of God" (James 2:23).

The story of Lot and his family can be read profitably next to that of Abraham. Lot, too, was wealthy (Gen. 13:5); he, too, showed hospitality to the avenging angels who came to Sodom, even to the extent of offering his daughters for ravishing to protect his guests (Gen. 19:8; cf. Judg. 19:22ff.). But when it was time to leave the city before the visitation of God's punishment, Lot "lingered; so the men seized him and his wife and his two daughters by the hand, the Lord being merciful to him, and they brought him forth and set him outside the city" (19:16). The angels make the choice clear to Lot's family: "Flee for your life; do not look back or stop anywhere in the valley; flee to the hills, lest you be consumed" (19:17). But, as we know, "Lot's wife behind him looked back, and she became a pillar of salt" (19:26). Why did she turn back? The Genesis account does not tell us, but the evangelist Luke has an interpretation of this incident in a series of sayings about the visitation of the Son of man (also to be cataclysmic, Luke 17:26ff.). In Luke's understanding, Lot's wife turned back in longing for the possessions she had left behind:

> Likewise as it was in the days of Lot — they ate, they drank, they bought, they sold, they planted, they built, but on the day when Lot went out from Sodom fire and brimstone rained from heaven and destroyed them all — so will it be on the day when the Son of man is revealed. On that day, let him who is on the housetop, with his goods in the house, not come down to take them away; and

likewise let him who is in the field not turn back. Remember Lot's wife. Whoever seeks to gain his life will lose it, but whoever loses his life will preserve it. (Luke 17:28-33)

Lot's wife, Luke suggests, was tragically confused. She identified her *being* with her *having*, her life with her possessions. She could not respond to God's call, and so lost the life that she sought to establish by what she owned. There is no doubt about the sharpness of Jesus' teaching here. "Whoever seeks to gain his life will lose it"; the Greek word used by Luke here *(peripoieo)* really means "to possess," and his point is simply that one who would try to hold onto life as a possession will lose it. The irony is that the loss comes not as the result of external punishment, but in the act of grasping itself. Life which comes from God cannot be seized and clung to as though it were ours.

Luke tells us another of Jesus' stories with a similar point, and about a person similarly confused:

[Jesus] said to them, "Take heed, and beware of all covetousness; for a man's life does not consist in the abundance of his possessions." And he told them a parable, saying, "The land of a rich man brought forth plentifully; and he thought to himself, 'What shall I do, for I have nowhere to store my crops?' And he said, 'I will do this: I will pull down my barns, and build larger ones; and there I will store all my grain and my goods. And I will say to my soul [life], "Soul, you have ample goods laid up for many years; take your ease, eat, drink, and be merry."' But God said to him, 'Fool! This night your soul [life] is required of you; and the things you have prepared, whose will they be?' So is he who lays up treasure for himself, and is not rich toward God." (Luke 12:15-21)

We notice in this passage that Jesus explicitly and emphatically rejects the identification of "life" with "abundance of possessions." It need not be pointed out that "abundance" can mean any quantity at all. The point is that the two are not on the same level, much less equal. The man in the story is not a fool because he is rich. He is a fool because he identifies his very existence with the security he thinks comes from having grain stored in barns. But his life is in God's disposition. The rich man's way of handling possessions symbolizes his way of treating his life: storing the possessions in secure places makes him feel that his existence is secure.

The story's bitter irony is found in the same symbolism at the end. The shattering of his life and the scattering of his possessions are both equally outside his control; "the things you have prepared, whose will they be?" (see also Ecclus. 11:18-19; Isa. 10:1-3; Ps. 49:6-8).

An important distinction should be made here. The distortion of reality that is idolatry makes things into gods. This is illusory. And the attempt to win life from possessions is folly. But this in no way suggests that things themselves are either illusory or evil. It is impossible to believe in the one God as Creator and regard his creation in any part as evil, or, for that matter, the use of any part of it as wicked. God approves of what he makes and finds it good (Gen. 1:31), and this approval extends to the use of creation given to Adam and Eve before the fall (Gen. 1:26-30). The Wisdom of Solomon asserts, "God created all things that they might exist, and the generative forces [or creatures] of the world are wholesome, and there is no destructive poison in them" (Wisd. of Sol. 1:14). The distortion of created reality is a consequence of the distortion of human freedom: "Do not invite death by the error of your life, nor bring on destruction by the works of your hands" (Wisd. of Sol. 1:12). In another passage, we find, "Thou lovest all things that exist and hast loathing for none of the things which thou hast made" (Wisd. of Sol. 11:24). As we have already seen, "possessing" is a fundamental aspect of human existence, because we are and have bodies. Given the way God has created us, and given the goodness of creation, it is inconceivable that the use of creation, and possessing, would be regarded as evil in and of themselves.

Against the false asceticism that would forbid marriage and the eating of certain foods, the author of 1 Timothy counters, "everything created by God is good, and nothing is to be rejected if it is received with thanksgiving" (1 Tim. 4:4). We understand, of course, that the "thanksgiving" does not *make* something good but only acknowledges it as good because it is from God. Nor is money a wicked thing by itself. Luke calls it "unrighteous mammon" to be sure, but precisely in that sentence in which Jesus tells his disciples to use it to make friends for the age to come (Luke 16:9). It is the serving of possessions as ultimate that is evil, and that prevents people from responding to the call from God. In Luke 16:13, Jesus says, "You cannot serve God and mammon." In this saying, mammon stands precisely as personified, as an idolatrous power that one can serve instead of God (this becomes clear especially from verse 15). A popular Hellenistic proverb is cited in 1 Timothy 6:10: "the love of money is the root of all evils." But the trouble here is not with the "money" but with the "love." It is the self-aggrandizing use of money that renders it idolatrous. Currency is indeed a human invention, but only when it is worshiped does it become "the work of human hands" as an idol. The degree of idolatry involved is revealed by the degree of resistance to the call of the true God. Immediately after Jesus spoke these words about serving God and mammon, Luke notes, cryptically, "The Pharisees, who were lovers of money, heard all this, and they scoffed at him" (Luke 16:14).

It is also important to note that material wealth is not by itself a wicked thing, or necessarily either the result or sign of an idolatrous pattern of living. This is particularly important to remind ourselves of given the tendency, noted in the introduction of this book, to shift imperceptibly from the concept "rich" to the concept "rich oppressor." Just as it does not take a great quantity of possessions to make an idol, so the simple fact of material wealth, however much extended, does not itself create an idol, as Abraham has shown us. Indeed, in that part of the Wisdom tradition in which the Deuteronomic principle of blessing and curse is rigidly maintained, wealth is seen as a straightforward sign of God's blessing. The Wisdom teachers had to struggle, as we do, with the tension between tradition and experience. The tradition was this: if prosperity in the land is one of the blessings that accompany the keeping of the covenant (Lev. 26:3-13; Deut. 28:2ff.; 30:1ff.), it makes sense to conclude that virtue and riches go together (Pss. 1:3; 25:13; 34:10, 17; 36:8; 37:3-4, 11, 22, 25; 112:2-10; 128:1-6; Prov. 3:10; 8:18-21; 13:22-23; 16:20; 22:4; 28:25) and that poverty is a result of foolishness if not of sin (Prov. 6:11; 10:4; 12:11, 27; 13:4, 18; 19:15; 20:4, 13; 21:17, 20; 23:21; 24:30-34; 28:19; Ecclus. 19:1). Within this perception, even if the wicked do seem to prosper (Ps. 10:5ff.), the conviction remains strong that they will also be punished (Pss. 1:4; 7:4-5; 10:15; 11:6; 34:21; 37:1, 9, 20, 28; 55:23; 58:6-11; 63:9-10; 68:2; 75:7-8; 92:7; Prov. 2:22; 3:33-35; 4:19; 5:22; 10:16, 30; 11:5, 21; 12:7, 21; 13:9; 15:24-25; 21:12; 24:20; 28:18; Wisd. of Sol. 5:8-14; Ecclus. 10:8; 12:3; 40:13; 41:1-2).

This conviction was, of course, heartily tested by personal experience and observation, and even within this conservative Wisdom tradition, the Deuteronomic equation is broken somewhat by the proposition that wisdom (i.e., virtue), even when accompanied by poverty, is better than the combination of wealth with wickedness (Pss. 19:10; 37:16; 119:14, 72; Prov. 3:14-15; 8:10-11, 19; 11:4; 15:16; 16:16, 19; 17:1; 19:1, 22; 20:15; 22:1; 28:6, 11; Wisd. of Sol. 7:8-14; 8:5-18; Ecclus. 10:23; 30:14-16; 40:25-26). The experience that so tested the Deuteronomic principle regarding possessions was the existence of oppression and the observation that many in the land were wealthy at the expense of others. The issue of oppression and unjust wealth is one I will turn to explicitly in the next chapter, for it is critical.

In itself, however, wealth is seen as a good (Ecclus. 13:24), so long as it does not result from the oppression of the needy (Prov. 1:12-13; 10:2; 11:16-18; 14:31; 20:17; 21:6; 22:16, 22-23; 24:15; 28:8, 20; Wisd. of Sol. 2:1-12; Ecclus. 4:1; 5:8; 7:3, 18, 20; 21:4, 8; 34:18-22) or become a false source of security or hope (Pss. 33:16; 49:6-8; 52:7; 62:9-10; 73:16-20; 146:3-4; Prov. 11:28; Wisd. of Sol. 13:10; Ecclus. 5:1, 8; 11:18-19; 18:25-26; 31:5-11). Not only is the conviction expressed, "Good things and bad, life and death, poverty and wealth, come from the Lord" (Ecclus. 11:14), but there is also within this tradition the perception that poverty and wealth are each in their fashion a testing of faith from God:

> Two things I ask of thee; deny them not to me before I die: Remove far from me falsehood and lying; give me neither poverty nor riches; feed me with the food that is needful to me, lest I be full, and deny thee, and say, "Who is the Lord?" or lest I be poor, and steal, and profane the name of my God. (Prov. 30:7-9; cf. Lev. 19:11-12)

In contrast to the wife of Lot, who confused her life and her possessions, is the example of the rich man Job. When stripped of all but bare existence, he declared, "the Lord gave, and the Lord has taken away; blessed be the name of the Lord" (Job 1:21). Job had not gotten his wealth by oppression (31:13-22); nor did he confuse his great wealth with the true center of his being:

> If I have made gold my trust, or called fine gold my confidence; if I have rejoiced because my wealth was great, or because my hand had gotten much; if I have looked at the sun when it shone, or the moon moving in splendor, and my heart has been secretly enticed, and my mouth has kissed my hand; this also would be an iniquity to be punished by the judges, for I should have been false to God above. (Job 31:24-28)

Notice here the connection between covetousness and idolatrous behavior, again. Rather than hoard the money, Job shared his wealth (31:16-17) and showed profligate hospitality: "the sojourner has not lodged in the street; I have opened my doors to the wayfarer" (31:31-32). Job stands as another example of how one can be rich and still claim righteousness. Indeed, even though Job did not confuse the issue of his life and his material possessions, he did make another sort of claim to possession in his righteousness before God, but that consideration must wait until the next chapter.

In reflecting over the mystery of human owning in the light of faith in God, I have suggested that material things are good insofar as they are part of creation and that owning and wealth by themselves are not evil. The mystery of human owning enters the mystery of iniquity by way of the meaning attached to that which is possessed. Once the identification of life and possession is made, things become idols, and the human spirit held in bondage to them cannot respond to God's call. It is in this connection that we can begin to understand something of the simple point that underlies the multitude of mandates in Luke's writings. Luke knows that possessions are symbols of human freedom and that the way a person disposes of possessions symbolizes the way he or she responds to God's call.

The same call went out to the first disciples (Luke 5:11, 27) and to the rich ruler (18:22). The disciples left all they had and followed Jesus; the rich ruler went away sad. It was God's call itself that identified him as "rich" in the sense that he was unable to respond. It does not matter here that the disciples left "only" boats and nets and family, whereas the ruler had to leave "great wealth." As Peter reminded Jesus, the things they left were, after all, "their own things" (Luke 18:28), no less dear to them for being ordinary, and certainly no less precious than the ruler's money. It was no easier leaving them because they were small; in fact, it may have been harder. But they left them. And why? It is critical to note in this connection that the disciples did not leave their homes and families and businesses because these things were evil and needed to be rejected for the sake of an ascetic ideal. Their response, like that of Abraham to the call from God to leave home and family for a strange land, was the response of obediential faith. Like Abraham, they only perceived the call dimly at first, certainly nothing of its consequences. But in the moment the call came, they discerned that it was a call to move out of their own project into that of another, and trusting him who called them, they obeyed. They were able, in spite of all their dullness and insensitivity, to believe at least this: their real life lay not with what was left behind, but with him who called them forward. The rich ruler, on the other hand, stands within Luke's narrative in decided and deliberate contrast to still another figure, the rich ruler of tax collectors, Zacchaeus, whose great wealth did not prevent him from responding to the visitation of the Messiah, welcoming him to his home, and giving enormous alms to the poor (Luke 19:8).

In the parable of the great banquet (Luke 14:16-24), which we are to understand as the image of the call to God's kingdom (see 14:15), the master's anger did not result from the fact that those who were first invited but refused to come *had* possessions, but that they allowed their involvement with these possessions to become so entangling that they could not respond even to this special invitation. Here is an interesting thing: the first two invited refused because of the demands of their possessions (field and oxen); the third refused the invitation because he had married a wife (14:20). In Jesus' teaching to the crowd immediately following this parable, he begins by saying that anyone who is so wrapped up in familial obligations that he or she cannot leave them behind, cannot be his disciple (14:26); he concludes, "whoever of you does not renounce all that he has cannot be my disciple" (14:33). In similar fashion, those who ran up to Jesus on the road wishing to become followers of his but wishing first to tend to familial obligations were rebuked by him (Luke 9:57-62). We see, then, that the renunciation of possessions is a function of responding to God's call; the shape and occasion of that call require discernment, if the proper disposition of possessions is to be made. One thing is certain — the inability to respond is revealed dramatically by the clinging to possessions.

The last passages I cited are important for another reason. We see in them that the issue of possessiveness is scarcely restricted to material things like boats and nets, stocks and bonds. In the same way that we can perceive and use things as though they were ultimate and the source of our identity and worth, so it is possible for us to lay claim to relationships as though they were possessions. Our ordinary language is again revealing. We say, "I have a wife," "I have a friend," "I have a fan club." We can reduce the mystery of human knowing and loving, trusting and sharing, to the language of money in the bank. The number of our acquaintances as surely as the number of our bank account, the roar of applause as surely as the roar of an outboard motor in our ears, the title of our spouse as surely as the title to our house can become the measure of our status and worth.

More subtly and perniciously still (because the counterfeiting is more clever), we can identify ourselves with our "spiritual" possessions: our ideas and visions, our time and energy, our dignity and virtue. These, too, can be clung to as though they were "us." They can become part of an idolatrous pattern of compulsive closure to the call of faith, which always bids us to move out of the world of our self-preoccupation into the concern of another.

How bereft am I when someone "steals" my ideas and uses them without acknowledgment? What diminishment of my very being do I experience when someone offends my dignity? How affronted am I when someone demands of me attention and time I had allotted for myself? So refined and complex are the varieties of spiritual self-aggrandizement that we are astonished at the tangled condition of the human heart in its quest for idols. The names for self-aggrandizement are legion. It is because this level of self-aggrandizement is not adequately taken into account that so many programs for the sharing of material possessions fail. It is not simply that humans, because we are bodies, will always be possessors. The difficulty is also that the elimination of all material possessions but the body by no means eliminates the idolatrous spirit within the human heart. It simply does not follow that because a person has few material possessions, he or she is "spiritually poor." I can cling as stubbornly to my theology as you to your automobile, to my asceticism as you to your orgy, to my virtue as you to your vice when I identify any of these as the source of my worth.

Now that we have cut down to the level of spiritual self-aggrandizement, and have recognized that the question of possessiveness goes far beyond the use of material possessions alone, it is appropriate to turn, finally, to that part of the Christian perception of reality that is specifically Christian — to look to the difference made by Jesus for our faith in God and the use of possessions.

The Faith of Jesus: The Poverty of Obedience

Christian conversion means turning away from idols as the measure of our worth to "serve a living and true God" (1 Thess. 1:9; Heb. 6:1; Gal. 4:8ff.). This conversion involves a different way of measuring ourselves: "As obedient children, do not be conformed to the passions of your former ignorance, but as he who called you is holy, be holy yourselves in all your conduct" (1 Pet. 1:14-15). This statement in 1 Peter recognizes that human behavior does fashion itself according to a pattern, and that this pattern (to which we "conform") itself derives from our fundamental perception of what is ultimate in reality. The "passions of your former ignorance" in this passage are shorthand for the way of life that characterizes idolatry (see 1 Pet. 1:18), which is, in turn, the perception of "the world." It will be understood that the meaning of "the world" in passages such as these lies not in a cosmological or anthropological referent but in an axiological one; "the world" signifies a whole system of perceptions and measurements characteristic of life organized apart from the recognition of the true God. So Paul says that conversion demands a transformation of this kind of perception: "Do not be conformed to this world but be transformed by the renewal of your mind" (Rom. 12:2).

This renewal of the mind does not take place through a willed adjustment of thought or by the persuasion of an argument. It comes about as the free gift from God of the Holy Spirit (Rom. 8:1-27), and the transformation of the human consciousness finds its new pattern in the image of the "new man," who is Jesus Christ, the exemplar of human faith and freedom (cf. Col. 3:10 with 1:15). The Christian is able to appropriate this new image of humanity, this new perception of the world and self before God, only because the human spirit has already been touched by grace, that is, the gift of God's Spirit (Rom. 5:5): "Now we have received not the spirit of the world, but the Spirit which is from God, that we might understand the gifts bestowed on us by God" (1 Cor. 2:12). And because of that gift "we have the mind of Christ" (1 Cor. 2:16). The Christian identity is one that is shaped by progressive response to the work of the Spirit in the heart of the Christian (the continuing response of obediential faith), whereby faith allows the "image" of the new humanity to be etched ever more deeply, integrally, and pervasively into the freedom of the believer: "Now the Lord is the Spirit, and where the Spirit of the Lord is, there is freedom. And we all, with unveiled face, beholding the glory of the Lord, are being changed into his likeness from one degree of glory to another; for this comes from the Lord who is the Spirit" (2 Cor. 3:17-18).

If the source of life before God is recognized as God's Spirit, then the norm of Christian existence is that provided by the Spirit: "If we live by the Spirit, let us also walk by the Spirit" (Gal. 5:25; cf. Rom. 8:13-14). That to which the Spirit conforms us is not a written code, but a living presence: "be renewed in the spirit of your minds, and put on the new nature, created after the likeness of God in true righteousness and holiness"

(Eph. 4:23-24). This new nature, this "likeness of God" which forms the pattern for the Spirit's etching, is none other than Jesus Christ, the "image of the invisible God" (Col. 1:15), and the perfect realization of that humanity created first in God's image (Gen. 1:26), the measure of mature humanity (Eph. 4:13). This is the whole of Christian anthropology — Jesus Christ.

Christians not only confess Jesus as Lord by the Spirit which comes from God (1 Cor. 12:3; Rom. 10:9), or acknowledge him as the effective cause of their salvation (Rom. 3:21-26; Heb. 7:24-25; 1 Pet. 1:19; 2:24; 1 John 1:7), but also see in him the model of authentic humanity before God. If we look to Adam for the pattern of disobedience and rebellion, we look to Jesus for the pattern of the human response of obediential faith to God (Rom. 5:12-21). Paul says of him, "For the Son of God, Jesus Christ . . . was not Yes and No; but in him it is always Yes. For all the promises of God find their Yes in him. That is why we utter the Amen through him, to the glory of God" (2 Cor. 1:19-20). Jesus is the final yes of God to humanity — for in him the promise to Abraham finds its unexpected but appropriate fulfillment (Acts 3:25-26; Gal. 3:14-16, 22; Rom. 15:8); and Jesus is the final yes of humanity to the Father — for in him, God's call was resoundingly answered with "Here I am, Lord." It is because the whole life of Jesus spelled this yes to the Father that Christians can say "amen" (that is, yes) to God. Insofar as Jesus sums up the gospel in his own person, we can suggest that Paul's "from faith to faith" in Romans 1:17 has the same meaning. In Jesus, God's faithfulness to his promise has been demonstrated; in Jesus, the response of faith has been perfectly enunciated.

Jesus is the "pioneer and perfecter of our faith" (Heb. 12:2). He is perfecter because he alone has, in his life and death, spoken an unequivocal yes to the Father:

> When Christ came into the world, he said, "Sacrifices and offerings thou hast not desired, but a body hast thou prepared for me; in burnt offerings and sin offerings thou hast taken no pleasure. Then I said, 'Lo I have come to do thy will, O God,' as it is written in the roll of the book." . . . And by that will we have been sanctified through the offering of the body of Jesus Christ once for all. (Heb. 10:5-7, 10)

He is pioneer because he has gone before us as scout to open the way for those of us who are to follow, so that we too can approach the throne of

God's mercy with boldness (Heb. 10:20-22; 4:16; Rom. 5:2; Eph. 2:18). This is the real significance of Paul's affirmation that "we have the mind of Christ." The Spirit which impelled the human person Jesus to perfect faith in God is the *same Spirit* (same principle of life) which impels us. "Because you are sons, God has sent the Spirit of his Son into our hearts, crying, 'Abba! Father!'" (Gal. 4:6). The terror that moves us to the compulsive self-grasping of idolatry is removed (at least potentially and insofar as it is received in faith) by this gift: "You did not receive the spirit of slavery to fall back into fear, but you have received the spirit of sonship. When we cry 'Abba! Father!' it is the Spirit himself bearing witness with our spirit that we are children of God" (Rom. 8:15-16; cf. Heb. 2:14-15). With this gift of the Spirit comes the gifts of freedom (2 Cor. 3:17; Rom. 8:2; Gal. 5:1, 13) and of genuine hope (Rom. 5:1-5; Col. 1:5; Heb. 6:19-20; 1 Pet. 1:3, 21) — freedom from the need to construct our own identity in idolatrous slavery to possessions of every sort, and freedom to bestow ourselves in response to the needs of others (Gal. 5:13ff.; 6:2); hope not in the transitory and illusory security of possessions, but in "God's love [which] has been poured into our hearts through the Holy Spirit which has been given to us" (Rom. 5:5). The overwhelming testimony of the New Testament is that, indeed, it "has been given to us," that the gift of God's Spirit is not only ideal, or extrinsic to us, but real, and genuinely impinges on human freedom in knowing and loving; that the human spirit can be and is transformed by the gift of the Holy Spirit responded to in faith. "Now when they saw the boldness of Peter and John, and perceived that they were uneducated, common men, they wondered; and they recognized that they had been with Jesus" (Acts 4:13).

Now, if the same Spirit which was at work in Jesus has been given to us, and if the Spirit is the one who enables us to say "Yes" to the Father in faith, then it follows that we are entitled to look to Jesus as the exemplar of our faith. The human faith of the man Jesus is the pattern of faith of the Christian. Theology has been hesitant in affirming this as boldly as it might, either because it has misunderstood the nature of obediential faith or because it fears that the reality of the incarnation is endangered once we allow that Jesus needed to be faithful as we need to or because it fears that anything that is done by a human being (even Jesus, even God's Son, and by the power of God's Spirit) ceases to be the work of God. These are groundless fears, and the neglect of the faith of Jesus has had disastrous effects on the development of Christian spirituality.

But the point of Jesus' humanity is that "he had to be made like his brethren in every respect, so that he might become a merciful and faithful high priest in the service of God, to make expiation for the sins of the people. For because he himself has suffered and been tempted, he is able to help those who are tempted" (Heb. 2:17-18). And the point of the human faith of Jesus is not that his faith is like *ours,* but that, by the gift of *his* Spirit, ours might become like *his:* "Christ also suffered for you, leaving you an example, that you should follow in his steps" (1 Pet. 2:21). The growth of the Spirit's life in the freedom of the believer should lead more and more to the reading of the story of Jesus as the Christian's own story.

It is in the human faith of Jesus that we find the deepest dimensions of poverty and the disposition of possessions as the radical articulation of faith in God. When Paul encouraged the Corinthians to share their possessions with the poor of Jerusalem by means of a collection, he gave them this motivation: "For you know the grace of our Lord Jesus Christ, that though he was rich, yet for your sake he became poor, so that by his poverty you might become rich" (2 Cor. 8:9). It is likely that Paul is here referring to Jesus becoming human in the first place, so that we are to read the "rich" as the preexistent state of the Son, and the "poverty" as the incarnation. The taking on of the human condition itself, then, was a form of impoverishment for the sake of others. In another passage, Paul tells the Philippians, "Have this mind among yourselves, which you have in Christ Jesus, who, though he was in the form of God, did not count equality with God a thing to be grasped, but emptied himself, taking the form of a servant, being born in the likeness of men. And being found in human form he humbled himself and became obedient unto death, even death on a cross" (Phil. 2:5-8). Christ did not "grasp" his status as God's Son as a possession, but "emptied himself" by becoming human. As in the passage from 2 Corinthians the incarnation itself is seen as an impoverishment, a dispossession of wealth. But the Philippians passage goes even further. As a human being, Jesus' pattern of obedience continued. He became obedient even unto death. The paradigmatic emptying which was the incarnation was carried out in the faithful human obedience of Jesus to his Father in his life leading toward the cross. By dying on the cross, Christ became "a curse for us" (Gal. 3:13): "For our sake he made him to be sin who knew no sin, so that in him we might become the righteousness of God" (2 Cor. 5:21). Here is the final point of "not clinging to equality with God" — to suffer the death of a sinner and one accursed by God, both, says Paul, "for us."

Faith in God is both trust and obedience. Because we trust the

Word of the Father we are able to obey; by obeying we give articulation to the trust. Paul can characterize the whole response to the gospel succinctly as "obedience of faith" (Rom. 1:5). Faith is the obediential hearing of another's call. Because it is the hearing of another, it calls us outside our self-concern; because it obeys, it must overcome the inner resistance to this movement outside our own preoccupation. In the very act of obediential faith, we see the pattern of death and new life. I must allow my self-project to die if I am to enter into the project of another and live in it. But only God can call me at so deep a level. And when it is God who calls, the offer of life is eternal. The paradox of faith is that by allowing my self-definition to die, I enter through that very dying into genuine life. The movement of faith, then, is a movement through death to life. It is the progressive opening of the human spirit to the Spirit which is God's life. It is the direct opposite of that progressive closure of the human spirit which is the orientation of idolatry and sin. For the movement of faith, death, which appears as the final closure to human freedom, is, in reality (in faith), the final leap of freedom to its source. What appears to be the ending to human identity is, in reality (in faith), its perfect establishment.

This is the pattern of faith we find in the man Jesus. How is he the pioneer of our faith? "In the days of his flesh, Jesus offered up prayers and supplications, with loud cries and tears, to him who was able to save him from death, and he was heard for his godly fear. Although he was a Son, he learned obedience through what he suffered. . . ." And how is he the perfecter of that faith? "And being made perfect he became the source of eternal salvation to all who obey him" (Heb. 5:7-9). Jesus, though God's Son, "learned obedience through what he suffered," and the essential suffering was itself the response of obediential faith, the painful opening of the clutched heart to the call of God. As Abraham was called to another country, so are we — and so was Jesus.

Now it is clear that as a human being Jesus experienced the same inner resistance to this call as we do. He would have liked to live on his own terms, for this is the natural impulse of the human spirit. In the garden he called out, "Abba, Father, all things are possible to thee; remove this cup from me" (Mark 14:36). Jesus' faith would have been insignificant if he had not a project of his own desire from which God could call him. And it was an intense desire, this wish to live, and on his own terms. In Hebrews it says he prayed with "loud cries and tears" (Heb. 5:7); Mark says that Jesus was "greatly distressed and troubled" (14:33). We, too, recognize these signs of resistance. But whereas we say "No" or "Maybe," Jesus says "Yes": "yet not what I will, but what thou wilt" (Mark 14:36). He moved out of the most powerful desire for self-preservation into the sphere of his Father's freedom. He who declared, "Whoever seeks to gain his life will lose it, but whoever loses his life will preserve it" (Luke 17:33), lived out his own words. It is in the yes of Jesus to the Father in the face of his terrible death that we find the culmination of the whole movement of his human faith: "I have come to do thy will, O God" (Heb. 10:7); "he . . . became obedient unto death, even death on a cross" (Phil. 2:8).

As at the end, so at the beginning. It would be mischievous to denigrate or underestimate the significance of Jesus' temptations for his faith and for ours (see Heb. 2:18). The point of the temptations, of course, is that Jesus really could have chosen another way of being messiah. That self-project was available to him. As a man of his age, as a student of the Scriptures, as one aware of a unique call from God, he could not but have been powerfully moved by the desires of his fellows (and himself) for a glorious redeemer of his people (see John 6:14-15; Luke 24:21). The synoptic accounts of the temptations (Matt. 4:1-11; Luke 4:1-12; Mark 1:12-13) compress into one symbolic encounter what must have been testings to Jesus' obedience throughout his life. Was he to be the sort of messiah his fellows and disciples wanted, or the kind of messiah God wanted? And how was he to *know* what kind of messiah God wanted him to be?

Jesus did not, I think, have a pipeline to heaven or a blueprint for messiahs or a continual state of ecstatic awareness of God's will. His knowledge of the Father's will was limited, as is ours, by his human condition (see Mark 13:32). It was the experiences of his life that presented God's will to him, as they do to us. The prayer of Jesus at the critical points in his ministry (see Luke 3:21; 4:1; 4:42; 6:12; 9:28-29; 10:21; 11:1; 22:41) was not for show, but for discernment. Only by allowing his own desires to become silenced in the prayer of silence, could he hear the Word being spoken to him by God in and through the circumstances of his daily life. Because he *listened* in prayer, he could *hear* the Word in events. Because he had one like this listening to him, God could shape his project through those events, knowing that Jesus would hear his Word in the babble of pleas and protestations that surrounded him. Because Jesus moved in prayer out of his own desires into a stance of waiting upon God, he could, in the diverse demands of his experience, move out of his self-project into the needs of others. Because Jesus was one who discerned the shape of God's Word in the fabric of his moment-to-moment existence, he could respond "Yes." Now he responded with jubilation: "I thank thee, Father, Lord of heaven and earth, that thou hast hidden these things from the wise and understanding and revealed them to babes; yea, Father, for such was thy gracious will" (Matt. 11:25-26; Luke 10:21). And then he responded in agony, "not what I will, but what thou wilt" (Mark 14:36).

The poverty of Jesus is not to be found first in his lack of material possessions, for he and his followers seem to have received support from others (Luke 8:1-3) and had sufficient funds to help the poor (John 13:29). The poverty of Jesus is to be found first in his faith. It is, properly speaking, a theological poverty. He is the one among us who has refused to identify his life in what he had, but sought his life in God's will; he is the one among us who has not clung even to his identity as God's Son, but has emptied himself out in obedience to the Father, minute by minute, in response to the circumstances of his life. When he would preach, he was called to heal (Mark 1:37-45); when he would rest, he was called to teach (Mark 6:31-34); when he would teach, he was called to feed (Mark 6:35-44); when he would live, he was called to die (Mark 14:33-36).

Since the faith of Jesus consisted in the obedient hearing of his Father's Word, and since that Word came to him, not alone in prayer or in the study of the Scriptures, but in his encounters with other men and women, the obedience of his faith was *articulated* by his response to their needs. He placed himself as an attentive servant to others, precisely because this was the way he could be the "servant of Yahweh" (see especially Isa. 50:4-6). It was also the only way he could, as a human being, discover what being a servant of God meant in concrete terms. There is the profoundest agreement between the "for us" of Paul, and the Jesus of the gospel: "The Son of man also came not to be served, but to serve, and to give his life as a ransom for many" (Mark 10:45); "I am among you as one who serves" (Luke 22:27). Or, as Paul put it in another place, "Christ did not please himself; but, as it is written, 'The reproaches of those who reproached thee fell on me'" (Rom. 15:3).

Jesus was simple with the simplicity of faith. His was not the sort of simplicity that moves out of compulsion and tries to clamp a rigid program on life, allowing nothing but what is programmed to be heard. The simplicity of Jesus was that simplicity given by the freedom of faith. Because he was free from the need to seize his own identity, even by the project of his preaching ministry, he was able to respond to all the complexity of the demands made upon him with attention and care. He was able to answer the genuine needs of people, and not only their spoken needs, for he was able to see the truth of their situations. From this openness to reality as the revelation of God's Word, Jesus was "pure in heart" and did "see God" (Matt. 5:8), did discern the shape of God's utterance in the needs of those around him.

Because he was simple with the simplicity of faith, Jesus was available to others, able to see them as God's children — that is to say, as they were — because he had no need to possess them himself. It was in responding to them, in moving out of his own project into their needs, that Jesus articulated his "Yes" to the Father, for it was in their needs that the Father's voice was to be heard. The body language of Jesus is the touching of the sick, the embracing of the children, the breaking of the bread as his body, and the stretching of his arms on the cross. In him, the disposition of the self and the disposition of what was his became one. He from whose side flowed blood and water said, "I thirst" (John 19:28, 34).

Comment

There are a number of ways that one could move "toward a theological understanding of possessions." One could, for example, begin with the doctrine of creation, as found in the creed. The profession of faith in one God who is "maker of all things, visible and invisible" provides a splendid basis for thinking about God's exclusive "ownership" of all that exists — and therefore the necessarily nonultimate character of all human claims to having — as well as for thinking about the relationship between God and humans, as well as among humans themselves, as well as the human relationship toward all other creatures, in terms of gifts given, received, and shared. Such a starting point also has a precedent in patristic thinkers, who argued for the sharing of possessions on the basis of the truth that "the earth is the Lord's and the fullness thereof" (Ps. 24:1), and found private property a distortion of the common possession of things that God desires (see John Chrysostom, *On Matthew* 46, 4).

My approach in this chapter is explicitly drawn from Scripture rather than the creed, and focuses not on God's work of creation but on the human response to that creative activity. My starting point might be called theological anthropology as displayed above all in the narrative and prophetic portions of Scripture. The advantage to this approach is that it enables me to enter into the same "inner and outer" of human experience that is at the heart of the mystery of possessions. There is a deep consonance, then, between the symbolic expressiveness of the "body language" of faith or idolatry and that of sharing or clinging to possessions. Locating the discussion in the mystery of human freedom demands perceiving possessions not as a problem that can be solved once for all, but as a dimension of human existence itself — one from which we cannot detach ourselves in a false objectivity.

Just such a false objectivity is displayed, I think, when the issue is put in terms such as "the problem of poverty." Whenever we designate something as a problem, we make two assumptions. The first is that we address something that is potentially solvable. A mathematic problem is such precisely because it can potentially be solved mathematically. An engineering problem will yield at least potentially to engineering techniques. But poverty is simply not this sort of problem. Simply at the material level — leaving aside all the subtleties — there are too many and too complex causes for human poverty for the assumption that these causes can be eliminated by human effort. We may change the economic system, but we do not control the weather, war, famine, stupidity, ignorance, and other such "accidents" that contribute to the uneven distribution of human goods. The second assumption is that "poverty" is necessarily a negative, something that must in principle be resisted or "fixed." The fallacy here is the same as in the equation of suffering and evil. Some suffering (such as that I inflict unjustly on you) may be an expression of evil. But to make all suffering evil, I remove the possibility that suffering may freely be chosen (in behalf of others), a function of growth (to learn is to suffer), or simply a concomitant of sentient existence (since suffering is the pain of a sentient system in disequilibrium). What I say here of suffering applies even more to poverty. It can in fact be something positive, not only in the "spiritual" sense, but also as a condition of material existence.

The best part about my theological-anthropological approach in this chapter, I think, is the way it provides us with a Christological model for the faithful use of possessions. In the character of Jesus as it is displayed in the Gospels, we find the fullest expression of faith as radical obedience to God's will. Jesus is defined, not by his own project, not by the expectations of others, not by the fear of failure or a competition for success, but by the constant discernment of God's call to him in the particular circumstances of his engagement with others. Jesus' poverty, in turn, is not defined by his lack of possessions, but precisely by the acces-

sibility, availability, freedom, that his radical obedience to God alone enables: he can respond to the needs of others because he lives within the
gift of being that comes from God. The Jesus of the Gospels shows us that
the sharing of possessions in the fullest sense requires the simplicity, the
purity of heart, that wills one thing.

CHAPTER 3

Sharing Possessions: Mandate and Symbol of Faith

We began thinking about the use of possessions in the Christian life by looking at Luke-Acts, to see if we could derive a clear mandate from one New Testament writing. Our failure to do so pushed us to think in a more fundamental way about what it means to "have" something in the first place, what this has to do with being human (being spirits in limited but expressive bodies), and how it fits in with our other perceptions of reality. This enabled us to turn to the Scriptures, not as a rulebook, but as a body of witnesses to what it means to live a human life before a creating, sustaining, and saving God.

When we looked at the Scriptures in this way, we found a great deal being said about the way people use possessions, and the focus was not so much on the things themselves as what they meant for those who claimed them. We saw how possessions symbolized the response of humans to what they perceived as ultimate: whether an idol that enslaves its worshipers in their attempt to grasp life as a possession, or the true God who calls humans out of such fearful, compulsive self-grasping into a new life of freedom that enables them to use things without being owned by them. The response to this call of God to acknowledge his claim on us and the world as Creator, and the call to enter into the new spaces he opens before us, we have called Faith. The first and most fundamental meaning of possessions, then, is their expression of the human response of idolatry or faith before the mystery of existence. Possessions are not good or evil in themselves; they derive significance from the way they extend our bodies in the world and thereby symbolize and affect our response to reality. There is a very close connection, therefore, between self-disposition and the disposition of possessions.

As the response to God is the most fundamental of all responses, so this is the most fundamental symbolization of possessions. If we are filled with the terror of nonbeing and the threat of worthlessness, and see our lives as something we must construct and then possess; if the security given by things (no matter whether material or spiritual) is all we have as a god, then we have *no choice* but to cling to what we possess. We cannot detach ourselves from our possessions because they are *us,* the source of our identity and worth. On the other hand, if we are able to acknowledge that our life comes at every moment from God, that we are held out of nothingness as a gift from him, that our identity and worth are established, not by what we can seize, but by what has been given to us in grace, then we need not define ourselves by what we own (materially or spiritually). We are freed for the first time from the tyranny of possessing. We are freed from the distortion of idolatry and can see all things as they really are — neither gods, nor the measure of human worth, but gracious gifts from the hand of God.

Authentic Christian poverty, then, is theological poverty, according to the pattern wrought in the human spirit by Jesus' example and gift. It is an essential articulation of faith as obediential hearing, which allows us to step out of the narrow space of self-definition into God's immense freedom. In this poverty, we do not cling even to our virtue as a possession. This is where Paul's teaching on justification by faith is so important, indeed critical. If there is any topic for which this teaching of the Apostle is pertinent it is that of human owning and being; if there is any place in the teaching of the Apostle where he comes closer to the heart of what Jesus' own obediential faith signified about human beings before God, it would be hard to find.

Paul sees that the human impulse to self-aggrandizement is so deep, devious, and pervasive, that even belief in the true God can be seized as a form of self-justification. I can seek to possess God's gracious love by the keeping of his law. I can seek to establish my own worth (righteousness) before him precisely by the punctilious performance of the commandments, even those that tell me to share my possessions with others. This is a highly refined mode of idolatry and the deadliest. If I can win God's favor by what I do for him, if my virtue can compel his recognition of me as righteous, then I worship a god who can be manipulated. I have brought the true God down to the level of an idol. Paradoxically, I am doing what Paul described as knowing God but refusing to acknowledge him as God or give him glory (see Rom. 1:21).

If my worth is established by my good deeds, then I have room to boast (Rom. 3:27; 4:2; Eph. 2:9). But such boasting is not only a form of rebellion, it is also a form of folly, for it denies the truth of our radical, and inescapable (and *continuing*), dependence on a God whom we cannot grasp and cannot even adequately name. Our God is not only the one who "gives life to the dead and calls into existence the things that do not exist" (Rom. 4:17), he is also the one who "chose what is low and despised in the world, even things that are not, to bring to nothing things that are, so that no human being might boast in the presence of God. He is the source of your life in Christ Jesus, whom God made our wisdom, our righteousness and sanctification and redemption; therefore, as it is written, 'Let him who boasts, boast in the Lord'" (1 Cor. 1:28-31; cf. Jer. 9:23-24).

God's way of making humans righteous (that is, establishing their worth before him) has been manifested apart from the sort of worth that human beings can claim for themselves even by the keeping of God's law, "For no human being will be justified in his sight by works of the law" (Rom. 3:20). God's way has been manifested in the emptying out, the impoverishment, of his Son, in the paradox of a crucified messiah. It is by the faith of Jesus, and by faith in Jesus as Lord (Rom. 3:22), that human beings are made righteous before God. This does not mean that "faith" is one more, if subtle, form of "work" or possession. It is an acceptance of, and an acknowledgment of, the one who works in us and possesses us. Faith does not, somewhere down the line, turn into a new form of "works" (Gal. 3:1-5), for that would be another way to idolatry (Gal. 4:8-11). Faith is the beginning and the end point of human response to the Good News from and about God: "For in it the righteousness of God is revealed through faith for faith; as it is written, 'He who through faith is righteous shall live'" (Rom. 1:17; cf. Hab. 2:4).

As God has established us in being as a gift, so has he restored us to worth before him through the gift of grace: "by grace you have been saved through faith; and this is not by your own doing, it is the gift of God — not because of works, lest any man should boast" (Eph. 2:8-9). Because God justifies us by his grace and we respond to that gift, not by acquisition but by faith, we are not only freed to be creatures, but God is allowed to be God, the sovereign power whose freedom alone can make us free.

With God, Paul tells us, there is no respecting of appearances (Rom. 2:11). In the judicial context from which this image derives (see, for example, Lev. 19:15), God's impartiality means that he cannot be bribed, even by the virtue of human beings. Herein lay the possessiveness of Job. As we saw in the last chapter, Job did not cling to his material possessions. But he stubbornly insisted on his own righteousness, his worth before God on his own terms. He wished to enter into litigation with his Maker, to plead his case, to force God into a fair hearing concerning Job's worth. But Elihu told Job:

> "If you have sinned, what do you accomplish against him? And if your transgressions are multiplied, what do you do to him? If you are righteous, what do you give to him; or what does he receive from your hand?" (Job 35:6-7)

Elihu suggested precisely that Job thought he could bribe God, and so spoke out in defense of God's transcendence. Job could not bribe God with his righteousness, and when he entered into the whirlwind of God's presence (38:1ff.), Job recognized the difference between theology and theophany: "I had heard of thee by the hearing of the ear, but now my eye sees thee; therefore I despise myself, and repent in dust and ashes" (Job 42:5-6). In short, Job learned the hard way the difference between being creature and being Creator.

This is the same and constant defense Paul makes of the divine transcendence. If God is truly to be God in any serious fashion, then his way of making humans righteous before him cannot involve manipulation. The climax of Paul's teaching on justification by faith is reached in his paean to the majesty of God in Romans 11:33-36:

> O the depth of the riches and wisdom and knowledge of God! How unsearchable are his judgments and how inscrutable his ways! "For, who has known the mind of the Lord, or who has been his counselor?" (citing Isa. 40:13)

God's way of establishing us in worth is not available to our prediction or control. It remains mystery. Paul's next line vividly recalls the passage in Job we have just seen: "Or who has given a gift to him that he might be repaid?" We cannot bribe him who is no respecter of appearances. And why is this? Why is there this disparity between our relationship to God and that to any other creature? Because God is not a creature: "For from him and through him and to him are all things." The proper human response to the mystery of God, then, is "To him be glory forever. Amen" (Rom. 11:36; cf. 1:20).

To accept our worth from God as a gift, then, means to dwell in continual nakedness before him, in the most radical form of poverty. We stand before him always as ones who know what he knows: that our being and worth come from him alone, for by ourselves we fall into nothingness at every moment. Without this poverty, which is the essential asceticism of faith, *any* use we make of material or spiritual possessions can become a form of acquisitiveness, of self-aggrandizement. If we seek to justify ourselves before God by observance of law or mandate; if we give alms to the poor; if we give away all we possess; if we share all we have in common, in each case our motivation and striving may be precisely to *possess* in another form or at least at another level. It can be the compulsive striving of idolatry — to win worth and being, to have something of our own doing to show to God as a sign of our worth, won by our own sweat: "See, I have done this, you must reward me!" Without the poverty of faith, the very sharing of our possessions may turn out to be a form of bribery. It can be the bribery of others: "I give you this to gain your gratitude, to win among you the reputation for virtue, to seize the power over you a benefactor inevitably has." It can also be the bribery of God: "I have given you glory by my deeds, you must give me love."

On the other hand, if we stand before God with the poverty that is faith, then we need not cling to any of our possessions as a means of self-definition and self-justification. The consequences of this should be clear. We can, for the first time, use things freely. We can also, for the first time, share possessions with others in a variety of ways, without being existentially threatened. But this sharing moves, not out of a desire to possess in another form, but as a gesture of freedom. How this can be so we will discuss next. However, as I try to show that how we perceive God determines our perception of other people, and that how we respond to other people determines the way we respond to God, I would ask the reader to keep in mind this fundamental realization: when I speak about the perception of God, I mean precisely all that has been argued about idolatry and the obedience of faith in the previous chapter.

How We View God Determines Our View of Other People

There can be no serious consideration of an ethics of material possessions unless the place of material possessions for human existence is located squarely within the human response to God, that is, theologically. The way we perceive and respond to the ultimate reality gives shape to the way we perceive and respond to all other reality. How we view God affects in the most pervasive fashion the way we see ourselves, the world, and other people; and the way we deploy possessions will symbolize precisely these perceptions.

If we see ourselves as having been thrown into existence by the whim of a faceless fate and regard our lives and our worth as dependent on what we can construct and hold for ourselves, if we have no center to our being except in what we possess, then we must view the things of the world as the means by which we can establish our identity and worth. The things of the world are the raw material for the fashioning of my idol. I stand, therefore, in relation to the world as an aggressor, for only by seizing it can I know that I exist. The corollary of this is that other human beings are thereby *inevitably* seen as my competitors. We are, all of us, in a survival-of-the-fittest situation. There is, after all, only a limited amount of world to go around, only a finite number of things that can be consumed or possessed.

If the more I have the more I am (the stance of idolatry), then my worth is measured by what I possess. But in a world of limited resources, I can have (and therefore be) more, only when you have less. If the emptiness of my being is filled only by what I achieve, there is really no way for me to measure my existence (my "reality") except by *comparison* with the achievement of others. I must stack up what I have against the stacks of others, to see not only how much I have but how much I am. This is certainly true not only for material possessions but for all human striving and effort within idolatry as well. However, with material things our bodies start impinging more directly on each other; the signs are clearer. Whether we are all equally full or equally empty does not matter for me as idolater; in either case I am profoundly threatened. If I emerge out of nothingness only by what I can grasp and point to, the measure of my existence will always be relative to the possessions of others. My idols can survive, in a word, only by consuming others.

When the world is regarded as the means to worth, and when other people are defined as competitors for worth, and when the only way to measure the relative ranks of our being and worth is by what we possess, then my only logical response to other human beings is expressed in the body language of the clenched fist. The fist seizes what it can, closes fiercely upon it, protects it rigidly, and threatens any who would open it. To relax the hand, to relinquish my possession, to share what I have, means to diminish my very *being,* which is held in existence at all only by my acquisitive effort. To lose one of my possessions is to lose part of my *self.* Allowing others to share freely in what is mine means that I have no way of distinguishing myself from them; I lose my identity. We do not have to look far for the evidence of this attitude toward possessions, this manifestation of idolatry. It is all around us, and within us; the call of faith leads us constantly out of idolatry because the idolatrous impulse never sleeps. The banality of suburban consumer competition ("keeping up with the Joneses") is only the easiest form of idolatry to parody. A claim to national strength and "worth" based on an ever-growing gross national product (the very apotheosis of quantitative reduction) is only the same outlook writ large. In between are all the clashes between those defined in various ways as "haves" and those defined in equally various ways as "have nots." Whether the "have" is specified as money, prestige, dignity, ethnic identity, power, beauty, brains, personality, virtue, asceticism, or spirituality, the tune is the same.

Unless we recognize that the same competitive dynamic is going to be present wherever worth is equated with possession, wherever being and having are identified, we only succeed in transposing the conflict by eliminating money as the measure. Herein is the "naiveté" of Marxism. Marx considered that, once the self-alienation of belief in God and the self-alienation inherent in private property were overcome (and he saw full well the displacement involved in the identification of worth with material possessions), human society could at last establish individuals in the proper human freedom. The historical manifestations of Marxism, however, have shown that human possessiveness operates quite as readily with power as with property, and the "leveling of society" economically only opens the way for other and perhaps more frightening forms of acquisitiveness, as in the totalitarian power of the few over the many. Where there is no measure to humanity's worth except humanity itself, there will always be idolatry and, where idolatry, slavery.

The perspective on the world and other people given by faith in the true God is altogether different — as different as the image of the one who stole fire from the gods is from that of the one who came to cast fire on the earth, that is, between Prometheus and Christ. If our being and our worth do not derive from our own acquiring of the world, but from the gift of existence and acceptance (justification) from the one who is totally other than the world, but to whom the earth belongs, then we are able to view all of creation as fellow sharer in the gift of existence and other human beings not as competitors for worth but as concelebrants in thanksgiving. Having been enabled by the gift of God's Spirit to call the source of all being "Father," we are able to turn for the first time to other people and say, "my sister," "my brother." A brotherhood or sisterhood of humanity based solely on humanity is a romantic fiction; but one based on God's Fatherhood is sober reality — not a Utopian vision of what we might accomplish, but the way things already are if we would but acknowledge it.

If my worth cannot be established by what I do, but is already given freely by the one from whom all blessings come (James 1:17-18), so it is with you, as well. If my value does not reside in what I possess, neither does yours. You and I have no bone of contention between us. As I cannot add even the smallest measure to my existence by what I have (Luke 12:25), neither can you. Your being in the world is not a threat to me, nor is mine to you. My being cannot be diminished by what you own and wear and use; nor can yours be by what I eat and think and say. Freed from the fear of emptiness and worthlessness, I do not need to grasp a piece of the world to dominate you and so be sure of my being. Nor need you. If you and I are equally naked before God at the level of existence, so are we equally loved by him as Father, and therefore equally clothed in the only worth that matters. We are freed from the need to possess in order to be, and therefore for the first time we can share what we have with each other. Now, by sharing, I neither diminish my being nor add to yours, neither enhance your worth nor cheapen mine.

It may be worth noting here that the command in Luke's Gospel, "Sell your possessions, and give alms" (12:33), occurs in a context of sayings about fear of others and the care God has for his creatures (Luke 12:4-34). Immediately preceding this command is the affirmation, "Fear not, little flock, for it is your Father's good pleasure to give you the kingdom" (12:32). Because our worth comes not from what we can grasp, but from the gift God has given to all without stint, we are freed from fear; and since we are freed from fear, we are able to share. Now our bodies are able to loose the clenched fingers of the fist and extend the hand openly, expressing by our body this truth about the world: there is, ultimately, nothing to fear (Rom. 8:31-39).

How We Respond to Other People
Is the Way We Respond to God

Just as the perception of God determines our perception of the world, our place in it, and whether we should fear or trust other humans, so the call of God to faith in him is articulated by the way we respond to other people. We have seen the paradigm of this already in the faithful obedience of Jesus: how the Father's Word was spoken to him in the circumstances of his life. And by responding faithfully to them, Jesus was in fact responding to the Father. In this section, I want to show how this same connection dominates the entire scriptural witness regarding possessions. Possessions not only symbolize our fundamental response to God in faith or idolatry, but they do so precisely in the way we use them in response to other people. The hoarding or sharing of possessions, in a word, articulates the response of faith in God by articulating fidelity and trust and obedience toward other children of God. It is within this understanding that we can return to the mandate concerning the use of possessions in the Law, the Prophets, the Writings, and finally, again, the Gospel.

The Law

The laws of the Pentateuch concerning possessions derive their force from this — that they are articulations of the covenantal obligations of the people of Israel toward each other because of their shared covenantal relationship with Yahweh. Fidelity to the covenant was expressed by fidelity to the laws that spelled out the demands of covenant. Because Yahweh was the Father of this people and called them into being, the Israelites were able to perceive each other as, and to call each other, brother and sister. This covenantal context for the laws is of first importance. The laws against oppression and injustice do not emerge from a Utopian program for human progress, or an egalitarian ideology, but from the demands of faith in the one God. Just as the keeping of the laws concerning possessions spelled out the people's allegiance to the one God who created, called, and established them as a people, so did their refusal to observe these laws manifest their apostasy from Yahweh and their turning to idolatry (see Exod. 20:1-4, 23; 23:13; 32; Lev. 19:4; 26:1-2; Deut. 4:15-20, 23-24, 28; 5:6-8; 6:13-14; 7:25-26; 12:30-31; 29:16-20).

The land in which the Israelites dwelt was regarded as the gift of the God who had called them out of bondage in Egypt. It was his to give because he was Creator of all things. It was a gift given to all the people. And as the people had no claim to existence except by the call of Yahweh, so did they have no claim to the land except as it came as a gift from God. This is the essential point: not only is Yahweh, as Creator, Lord of all the earth (Deut. 10:14-15), he is, as Creator of this people, the only real possessor of the land of Israel: "The land shall not be sold in perpetuity, for the land is mine; for you are strangers and sojourners with me. And in all the country you possess, you shall grant a redemption of the land" (Lev. 25:23-24). The land that was given to the people as an inheritance to fulfill the promise to Abraham (Deut. 6:10) was for their use, but not for their keeping. It was, first of all, the dwelling place of the Lord, and sacred to him (Num. 35:34). The Israelites could no more lay ultimate claim to the land than they could to their own life-breath; it came as a constantly renewed gift.

As they came into this inheritance because of the covenant freely established with them by God, so the way they lived in the land (the way they handled this possession) indicated their fidelity, or lack of it, to that covenant. So directly did the disposition of the land symbolize the relationship with Yahweh, that the practice of letting the land lie fallow on the seventh year could be called a "sabbath of the land" (Lev. 25:1-7). Specifically, it was the way the Israelites used the property either to hurt or to help their fellows that indicated in a concrete fashion whether they clung to Yahweh as the source of their life or to idols.

The prosperity that the land could yield might itself lead to their forgetting the source of its prosperity:

> "Take heed lest you forget the Lord your God, by not keeping his commandments . . . lest, when you have eaten and are full, and have built goodly houses and live in them, and when your herds and flocks multiply, and your silver and gold is multiplied . . . then your heart be lifted up, and you forget the Lord your God, who brought you out of the land of Egypt, out of the house of bondage. . . . Beware lest you say in your heart, 'My power and the might of my hand have gotten me this wealth.' You shall remember the Lord your God, for it is he who gives you power to get wealth; that he may confirm his covenant which he swore to your fathers, as at this day. And if you forget the Lord your God and go after other

gods and serve them and worship them, I solemnly warn you this
day that you shall surely perish." (Deut. 8:11-19)

In this magnificent passage, the connection between self-aggrandizement
and idolatry is explicitly drawn, as well as the proper understanding of the
relationship of possessions to human worth: "it is he who gives you power
to get wealth" (see also Deut. 32:6-9).

Inasmuch as all the people called into covenant were to share in the
promise, all were to have a share in the land. The attention paid to the
precise allocation of land to the tribes (see Josh. 13–19; Num. 26:52-56)
has the theological understanding behind it that each Israelite was to
have some part of the land, given as a gift from God. The priestly tribe of
Levi alone did not share in this division: "To the tribe of Levi alone Moses
gave no inheritance; the offerings by fire to the Lord God of Israel are
their inheritance, as he said to him" (Josh. 13:14; cf. Num. 18:20-24; 35:1-8;
Deut. 18:1-8). The Levites, with their population spread throughout the
other tribes, depended for their support on their brother Israelites. Their
inheritance "was the Lord," and among the first obligations of the people
was to give a portion of their possessions to this dispossessed clan: "you
shall not forsake the Levite who is within your towns, for he has no portion or inheritance with you" (Deut. 14:27). For the rest, however, and ideally, each Israelite within each tribe was to enjoy that portion of the land
and its produce given as Yahweh's gift.

This view of the land itself as an inheritance, or as a free gift given in
fulfillment of the promise, had two implications. First, since the land
came as a gift, there was to be no collapsing of private property; there
was not to be indiscriminate use of the land by all. The warnings against
moving landmarks (Deut. 19:14; Prov. 22:28; 23:10) remind us that the limits of an individual's property had been set by God and were not to be
tampered with. Second, and out of the same perception, any attempt to
win prosperity by taking the property of another (in any way) was a direct offense against God, not alone because it broke a law, but because
the property of a neighbor came to him as a share in God's heritage.

The laws of the Pentateuch are nothing if not realistic. Just as the
command not to kill (Exod. 20:13; Deut. 5:17) did not eliminate the necessity of legislating for all possible varieties of homicide (Exod. 21:12-15;
Deut. 19:4-13), or the command not to steal (Exod. 20:15; Deut. 5:19) relieve the burden of deciding property restitution of every sort (Exod.
21:26–22:12; Num. 5:5-8), so also the promise of prosperity in the land did

not blind the legislator to the facts of life — some people were in fact poor, through no fault of their own, and needed legislation to protect them. The Levites were not the only "dispossessed" in the population. There were other groups who, within a patriarchal, land-based society, fell into the category of the needy; preeminent among them were the orphan, the widow, and the sojourner (resident alien). They represented the structural anomalies of the land-holding system, the ones who, once cut off from the inheritance of the land, needed to rely on others for support. The most constant and painstaking attention is paid to them in the laws dealing with possessions (see Exod. 22:21-22; 23:9; Lev. 19:9-10; 19:33; 23:22; Deut. 10:17-19; 14:28-29; 16:9-15; 24:17-18; 26:12-15). There is the recognition, therefore, that quite apart from the scheme of punishment for sin, poverty could come upon a portion of the people. Some of the laws are directed toward restoring property to those who are dispossessed and some toward alleviating perpetual need.

For landholders who had lost their property through bankruptcy, there was the mechanism of the Jubilee Year: "you shall hallow the fiftieth year, and proclaim liberty throughout the land to all its inhabitants; it shall be a jubilee for you, when each of you shall return to his property and each of you shall return to his family" (Lev. 25:10). The return of the property to its ancestral owners is explicitly and emphatically connected to Yahweh's ownership of the land (Lev. 25:23-24). Not only property indebtedness, but debts of every sort were to be canceled in the Jubilee Year (Lev. 25:29-42). In Deuteronomy 15:1-3, every seventh year is to be regarded as a year of release, when all debts are canceled and all slaves released (see Deut. 15:12-18; Exod. 21:2; Lev. 25:1-7). Israelites who, because of poverty, have had to serve other Israelites, were not to be held in perpetual servitude. Just as the land was the Lord's, so were all the people: "they are my servants, whom I brought forth out of the land of Egypt; they shall not be sold as slaves" (Lev. 25:42). The laws caution against craven calculation regarding the Jubilee Year by, for example, refusing a loan because the time of release was drawing near (Deut. 15:9) or unfairly adjusting the price in a sale because of this statute of limitations: "You shall not wrong one another, but you shall fear your God; for I am the Lord your God" (Lev. 25:17).

For those perennially impoverished because of their dispossessed status (orphans, widows, sojourners), the law demands a sharing in *the produce* of the land. There are diverse laws for this, undoubtedly reflecting different times, situations, and traditions; but the central perceptions and concerns remain constant. In Exodus 23:10-11, the sabbath of the land in the seventh year is seen as an opportunity for the "poor of your people" to eat from the produce yielded by the untended fields and vineyards. The law in Leviticus 19:9-10 states that in the harvesting either of grain or of grapes, the landowner is not to glean to the end of a field or strip the vines bare, but is to leave a portion for the poor and sojourner (see also Lev. 23:22; Deut. 24:19, and its exemplification in Ruth 2:3). Deuteronomy 14:28-29 stipulates that the tithes of every third year should be laid up in the towns, to be available for the support of the Levite, sojourner, orphan, and widow (see also Deut. 26:12-15). The tension between the ideal and the reality within Israel is admirably, if unconsciously, intimated in Deuteronomy 15:4-5 and 11. The ideal is stated in 15:4-5: "there will be no poor among you (for the Lord will bless you in the land which the Lord your God gives you for an inheritance to possess), if only you will obey the voice of the Lord your God. . . ." But, a little later, the reality is faced: "the poor will never cease out of the land" (Deut. 15:11). From this perception, and from the demands of the covenant, comes the mandate to Israel: "therefore I command you, You shall open wide your hand to your brother, to the needy and to the poor, in the land" (Deut. 15:11).

Another hard fact faced by the laws is the fact of sin. The laws recognize that some Israelites would not abide by the demands of the covenant regarding property and would seek prosperity at the expense of others. In addition to the straightforward means of stealing (Lev. 6:2; 19:11, 13), there were more subtle mechanisms of oppression available. Oppression could take the form of not allowing the poor to reap the fields (Exod. 23:9-11), of moving landmarks (Deut. 19:14; 27:17), of keeping in pledge what was needed by a poor man for survival (Lev. 6:4; Deut. 24:10-13), or of holding back wages from a laborer (Lev. 19:13; Deut. 24:14-15). An even more sophisticated means of dispossessing others was provided by the "perversion of justice" — using false weights and scales in measuring (Lev. 19:35; Deut. 25:13-16), bribing a judge to favor one's own cause, in a society where disputes were settled before judges, or, if one were the judge, taking such a bribe and "showing partiality" rather than judging the case on its merits (see Exod. 18:20-22; 23:2-8; Lev. 19:15; Deut. 10:17-19; 16:18-20; 24:17; 27:19). Whatever the precise manner, "oppression" and "the perversion of justice" are the basic sins against the neighbor regarding possessions in Israel.

What is most striking about the condemnation of this sort of oppression, however, is its theological placement; this kind of self-aggrandizement at the expense of others is seen as directly breaking covenant with Yahweh. It might be thought that oppression or the perversion of justice was, first of all, an offense against the neighbor, but Leviticus 6:2 calls all manner of oppression and deception a "breach of faith against *the Lord*." Breaking trust with the neighbor is breaking trust with God; our response to other human beings articulates our response to God. And, as idolatry is regarded as the alternative to faith in Yahweh, a close connection is also made in the Pentateuch between such oppressive and unjust behavior and idolatry. The laws against oppression in Exodus 20:24ff. are bracketed by warnings against idolatry in Exodus 20:23 and 23:32 (see also Lev. 25:55–26:2; Deut. 7:25-26; 29:16-20). The claim that idolatry leads to the murder of the innocent (Deut. 12:30-31) is literally true for oppression as an expression of idolatry: those who oppress the needy and poor have murder on their hands.

The laws provide different motivations for avoiding oppression and injustice, but they all are rooted in the relationship of this people to God. The people are to care for the sojourners, because they themselves were once sojourners: "Love the sojourner therefore, for you were sojourners in the land of Egypt" (Deut. 10:19; cf. Exod. 22:21; 23:9; Lev. 19:34; Deut. 24:17, 22). The implication of this, of course, is that Israel only enjoys the land now because "the Lord your God redeemed you from there" (Deut. 24:18). In fact, the sojourners and Israelites stand before God with equal status; both derive all they are and have from him. There is to be, therefore, but one law for sojourner and native alike (Lev. 24:22). Why? Because, "the land is mine; for you are all strangers and sojourners with me" (Lev. 25:23).

When God called Israel into being as a people, he redeemed those who were themselves oppressed (Exod. 2:23-25; 3:7-10). His power to "work justice" for the oppressed has not ceased. Those who oppress the poor will have to deal with God's avenging anger. If the poor, the widows, or the oppressed cry out to God, he will hear them and punish the oppressor (Exod. 22:21-27; Deut. 25:9). Those who pervert justice by taking bribes will have to deal with "the great, the mighty, and the terrible God, who is not partial and takes no bribe. He executes justice for the fatherless and the widow, and loves the sojourner, giving him food and clothing" (Deut. 10:17-18).

The ultimate motivation for doing justice and helping the needy was, therefore, the covenantal relationship with Yahweh. In Leviticus 19:1-37, where we find a concentration of laws dealing with oppression and injustice, we find the individual commands followed by the refrain, the flat assertion, "I am the Lord," or, "I am the Lord your God." Because Yahweh is the God he is, and because he is Lord of this people, they are to be holy as he is holy (Lev. 19:2); they are to measure themselves against God, and not against the specious power of idols (Lev. 19:4). Because God himself is the measure of their existence, they are not to oppress or work injustice (19:11-16); they are to leave a portion of the field for the poor and sojourner (19:10); and they are to use just weights and measurements (19:35-36). The section concludes, "I am the Lord your God, who brought you out of the land of Egypt. And you shall observe all my statutes and all my ordinances, and do them: I am the Lord" (19:36-37). In the heart of this section of the Law, we find the heart of the covenantal principle: "you shall love your neighbor as yourself." And why? Because "I am the Lord" (Lev. 19:18). The laws of the Pentateuch dealing with possessions express this truth: we respond to God through our neighbor.

The Prophets

The same theological perception shapes the context for the attacks of the prophets on the oppressors of the poor and those who pervert justice within Israel. In the prophetic writings, we find woes addressed to those who live in luxury because of their oppression of the poor (Amos 6:1, 4; Mic. 2:1-2; Isa. 3:16; 5:8, 11; 10:1-2; Jer. 22:13), who revel in mindless unconcern about God's visitation (Isa. 22:13), who foolishly trust in wealth to provide them with security (Zeph. 1:18; Isa. 10:3; 31:1-3; Jer. 2:11-13; Ezek. 7:19-21; 20:7ff.). With some regularity, the punishment of the wicked is symbolized by the destruction of the possessions in which they trusted (Hos. 9:6; Joel 3:5; Nah. 2:9; Zeph. 1:12-13; 2:15; Zech. 9:3-4; 14:14; Isa. 3:18-24; 5:9; 14:11; 42:22; Jer. 5:16-17; 6:12; 15:13; 17:3; 20:5; Ezek. 7:19-21; 23:26).

It should be noted that it is not wealth itself that is the object of prophetic fury, but wealth that has resulted from the oppression of others (Amos 3:10; 4:1; 8:4-6), stealing (Hos. 4:2; 7:1), or the perversion of justice (Hos. 10:13; 12:1). As in the laws, the two great prophetic categories for wrongdoing in property matters are oppression and the perversion of justice. In the prophets, too, a direct connection is drawn between infidelity to Yahweh and perfidy toward the neighbor. The prophets place before the people time and again the basic choice between keeping faith with Yahweh in covenant, to "know the Lord" (Jer. 9:6), and the following after idols (see Hos. 8:1-4; 13:1-4; 14:8; Zeph. 1:5-6; Mal. 2:10; Jer. 1:16; 2:11-13; 7:23-26; 11:1-13; 16:10-13; 18:15; 25:6; Ezek. 20:1-8). At times, the prophets immediately link apostasy and idolatry to the oppression of the poor (Amos 5:4-6 and 5:11; cf. Hab. 1:16; Jer. 2:27 and 2:34; Ezek. 16:49, 52; 22:1-8, 12, 25, 27, 29) and to the perversion of justice for wicked gain (Amos 5:4-6 and 5:12; cf. Isa. 1:21-23; Ezek. 18:10-13). It may be more than accidental that so much talk about idols is also talk about silver and gold (see Hos. 8:4; 13:2-3; Nah. 1:14; Hab. 2:18-19; Isa. 2:7-8, 20; 30:22; 31:7; 40:18-20; 41:7; 42:17; 46:5-7; Jer. 10:9; Ezek. 7:19-21).

The prophetic condemnation was directed at those who broke faith with Yahweh. Even when idols are not mentioned explicitly, the prophets consistently maintain that the breaking of covenant with Yahweh leads to and is directly expressed by the oppression of the poor and needy, sojourner and laborer, orphan and widow (see Amos 2:6-8; 3:2; Hos. 12:7-9; Mic. 3:1-3; Zeph. 1:9; 3:1-3; Mal. 3:5; Isa. 3:5, 14-15; 5:7-10; 30:12; 58:3; Jer. 5:25-29; 6:12-13, 19; 8:10; 9:4-6). The perversion of justice, too, is a direct result of an expression for breaking covenant with Yahweh (see Mic. 3:9-12; 7:3-6; Hab. 1:4; Zeph. 3:3-7; Isa. 1:4; 3:9; 5:23-24; 30:12; 59:4-15; Jer. 34:8-22; Ezek. 9:9). Conversion back to Yahweh, therefore, meant coming back to the covenant with him. This meant not only shattering the idols that had been the cause of apostasy (Mic. 5:13; Isa. 2:20-22; 26:13-14; 30:22) but also "doing justice" to and for those designated by the law of the covenant as needy, preeminently orphans and widows.

The Word of the Lord to those who had turned from him was, simply, "Keep justice, and do righteousness" (Isa. 56:1). This is spelled out in Zechariah 7:8-10: "Render true judgments, show kindness and mercy each to his brother, do not oppress the widow, the fatherless, the sojourner, or the poor; and let none of you devise evil against his brother in your heart." In other words, keep the laws concerning possessions in the law of the covenant, and you will be showing fidelity to the God of the covenant. Jeremiah interprets the punishment of Jerusalem: "Why has the Lord dealt thus with this great city? . . . Because they forsook the covenant of the Lord their God, and worshiped other gods and served them" (Jer. 22:8-9). And in an oracle shortly before the one just cited, Jeremiah states succinctly the demands of that covenant: "Do justice and righteousness, and deliver from the hand of the oppressor him who has been robbed. And do no wrong or violence to the alien, the fatherless, and the widow, nor shed innocent blood in this place" (Jer. 22:3; cf. 21:12).

Authentic conversion to Yahweh, in other words, was not a matter of cultic loyalty but of keeping the laws governing relationships among the people. Religious observance without the keeping of these laws was worthless in the eyes of God (Isa. 58:1-9). Doing justice and saving from oppression, we notice, are not just the passive avoidance of evil, but active; the people are to "save" from oppression and "do" justice in the land. This becomes almost a shorthand symbolization of conversion to Yahweh (see Hos. 12:6; Zeph. 2:3; Zech. 8:16; Mal. 4:4; Isa. 1:17; 33:15-16; 56:1-6; Jer. 7:5-7; 21:12; Ezek. 18:7-9). This is so simply because of the nature of the one who called them into covenant: "I the Lord love justice, I hate robbery and wrong" (Isa. 61:8); "I am the Lord who practices kindness, justice, and righteousness in the earth; for in these things I delight, says the Lord" (Jer. 9:24). In the preaching of the prophets, therefore, as in the laws of the Pentateuch, we see that the human use of possessions directly symbolizes and makes real the fundamental human response to God, and it does this precisely in the way possessions are taken from or given to other human beings. We respond to our neighbor as we respond to God. How we use possessions reveals both.

A final prophetic text might be read in this light. In Micah 6:6-8, we hear the human response to Yahweh's charge of apostasy from him (6:1-5). The prophet asks in anguish, "With what shall I come before the Lord, and bow myself before God on high?" The text goes on to ask whether God will be pleased if the human being offers him his best possessions, gives them up in sacrifice. Will God be placated by being offered calves or rams or oil? But maybe these external possessions will not suffice; maybe God demands of me the truncation of life in response to him; shall I offer "my first-born, . . . the fruit of my body?" The Word of the Lord which came to Micah, and through him to us, bypasses these grand gestures. The point of the theological focus of possessions is not that we give them up for God, but that we use them faithfully toward others, for in so doing we are responding to him; we are giving thanks for his creation. The Word says, simply, "He has showed you, O man, what is good; and what does the Lord require of you but to do justice, and to love kindness, and to walk humbly with your God?" (Mic. 6:8).

The Writings

The Writings have the same theological perception of oppression and injustice. The "wicked" in the Psalms are frequently designated simply as those who oppress the poor and prevent justice (Pss. 10:2, 9; 14:4, 6; 37:14; 43:2; 55:2, 11; 58:2; 71:4, 11; 82:2-4; 94:4-7; 109:16; 123:4; 140:4-5), or who take bribes and exact interest on loans (Pss. 15:5; 26:10). The psalmists frequently attach such oppression of the poor to the atheism of the fool or the wickedness of the idolater (see Pss. 10:3-4; 14:4; 16:4; 31:6, 13; 36:1; 40:4; 53:1-4; 59:6ff.; 64:5-6; 71:11; 73:4-13; 94:4-7).

In spite of the high valuation the Proverbs place on wealth, they explicitly reject prosperity gotten as a result of oppression. Oppression of the poor is wrong before God (Prov. 14:31; 24:15) and will be punished by him (Prov. 22:22-23). The same sanction is held over greed and the taking of bribes (Prov. 15:27; 21:14, 28), cheating in matters of property (Prov. 11:1; 16:11; 20:10, 23), and the perversion of justice (Prov. 17:15, 23; 18:5; 24:23-24). The theological perspective is sharply focused in Proverbs 17:5: "He who mocks the poor insults his Maker." Not only is right judgment to be shown to the poor and needy (Prov. 31:9), but the demand of the law extends to the positive helping of the poor. The good wife is one who cares for the poor (Prov. 31:20), just as the righteous man is one who gives and does not hold back (Prov. 21:26). In every circumstance, the person who has more is to share with the one who has less (Prov. 3:27-28; 25:21-22; 28:27; 29:7). This, it should be made clear, is not simply a matter of piety. The man who closes his ear to the cry of the poor will find God's ear closed to his own pleas (Prov. 21:13). Proverbs 21:3 declares, "To do righteousness and justice is more acceptable to the Lord than sacrifice," and in Proverbs 19:17 there is this astonishing assertion: "He who is kind to the poor *lends to the Lord,* and he will repay him for his deed" (italics added).

In Ecclesiasticus (Sirach) as well, there is the clear prohibition of oppression in any form (Ecclus. 4:1; 7:20), and of partiality in judging (4:9, 22, 27; 7:3; 42:1-4). Again, the theological warrant for this is direct; the *Lord* shows no partiality and hears the cry of widow and orphan (35:13-14), and the prayer of the poor person goes directly from his lips to God (21:5). Injustice is odious to the Lord (10:7), for he is a God who helps the poor (11:12-13) and demands the same from us. There is a passion to some of Sirach's observations that raise his sayings to the level of prophetic oracle:

> The bread of the needy is the life of the poor. Whoever deprives them of it is a man of blood. To take away a neighbor's living is to murder him; to deprive an employee of his wages is to shed blood. (34:21-22)

If oppression is murder, offering sacrifice to God with the possessions gotten from oppression is blasphemy: "Like one who kills a son before his father's eyes is a man who offers a sacrifice from the property of the poor" (34:20).

It is not enough to keep from oppression and injustice; covenant with God demands that we deliver the oppressed (4:9); it is a sin to turn away one's face from the needy (4:4). We are, rather, to turn our ear to the cry of the poor (4:8; 29:8); if we do not, God will punish us (4:6). The teaching of Sirach is distinctive in the emphasis it places on almsgiving as a way of sharing possessions with the poor. I will return to the development of this tradition in Judaism in the next chapter, but for now I will note that Sirach stands at the head of that tradition which sees the giving of alms as the finest expression and fulfillment of the command to "do justice" (*sedeqah* = justice = almsgiving). Almsgiving is advocated in 3:30; 4:3; 7:10; 12:3; 29:9-13; and 31:11. It wins, says Sirach, a reward from God (17:22) and a blessing (7:32). It provides the best security for life (40:24); it endures forever (40:17), for it is an act of worship to God: "He who gives alms offers a thank-offering" (35:2).

We have seen many different mandates concerning possessions in the writings of the Old Testament. On the negative side, people are not to steal, cheat, "do injustice," or oppress others. Positively, the covenant demands that the poor and needy be helped by restoring them to their land, by leaving a corner of the field for gleaning, by lending without interest, by storing up third-year tithes in towns for the poor, and by almsgiving. There has been no trace of an ideal of community possessions; I will return to this.

In spite of this multiplicity of mandates, the basic perception of the Old Testament as a whole regarding possessions is quite clear and straightforward — material things are important as signs of our self-disposition. If we recognize that we and all that we have are gifts from God, we will respond to his covenant with justice and care for our fellow humans. If we refuse to acknowledge this dependence on God, we will make an idol of possessions and do evil to our fellow humans in order to gain ascendancy over them. What we found by means of reflection in chapter 2, therefore, we here find verified in the Scriptures. The way people use possessions articulates their response to God. If they respond by idolatry, then the movement is toward self-aggrandizement, oppression, and injustice; if by faith, the movement is toward appropriate sharing of possessions with others according to their needs. The command to love

the Lord with all the heart is given content by the command to love one's
neighbor as oneself.

The Letter of James

The New Testament Letter of James continues the witness of the Law,
Prophets, and Writings to the church of Jesus Christ. James contrasts authentic faith in God, which, like Abraham's, makes the believer a "friend
of God" (James 2:23), with that "dead faith" (2:17) which is simply ritualis-
tic and camouflages an orientation to life that reveals one as in "friendship with the world" (4:4). James asserts clearly that the way people respond to other human beings, "who are made in the likeness of God"
(3:9), is the way they respond to God.

Being a "friend of the world" means being at "enmity with God" (4:4).
It is important, if we wish to understand properly this sharp statement,
to remember what was meant by "friendship" in James's time. To be a
friend of someone meant to "be of one soul" with another, and to "have
all things in common" (this will be picked up in the next chapter). What
this means, concretely, is that friends have a shared perception of reality
and a "likeness" of attitude and behavior. Now, when we also remember
that "the world," as so frequently in the New Testament, refers to a whole
system of values apart from belief in God, it is clear what James intends.
Being a friend of the world means measuring oneself by the frame of the
visible world as closed to God, a frame characterized by hostile passions
(3:16). To be of "one mind" with this world means to refuse to acknowledge God's claim on us.

The reality is this: everything that exists comes into being as a gift
from God; he is the one source of life and worth (James 1:17-18). But it is
possible to deceive oneself (1:16) and to base one's life, not on thanksgiving to God, but on compulsive desire (1:15). James accurately attrib-
utes the wars and conflicts between peoples to the competitive clash of
ruthless desire: "You desire and do not have; so you kill. You covet and
cannot obtain; so you fight and wage war" (4:2). It is not by accident that
the use of possessions by people who are so enslaved by desire is marked
by oppression and injustice. The one who is a friend of the world is filled
with an arrogance and self-aggrandizement that is at odds with faith in
God (4:16 and 4:6-10). Out of this arrogance, the acquisitive person op-

presses the poor and drags them into court (2:6) and defrauds laborers of their wages (5:4).

But those who seek to establish their lives on the basis of what they can gain and possess are fools. They are not even able to account for tomorrow's breath, much less next year's profit; yet they go on about their projects as though they were secure. James asks them, "What is your life? For you are a mist that appears for a little time and then vanishes" (4:14). The rich man fades away "in the midst of his pursuits" as surely as a flower scorched by the heat (1:11). There is certainly not much room for boasting in this. James wants us to realize that the same sort of worldly orientation is possible for the Christian who professes verbally "the faith of our Lord Jesus Christ, the Lord of glory" (2:1). The believer can, in fact, be "double-minded" (1:7), confessing one thing with the lips, but living his or her life by quite another measure. The real mark of authentic faith is the way we respond to our fellow human beings. And the norm for this response is "the royal law, according to the scripture, 'You shall love your neighbor as yourself'" (2:8). This "law of the kingdom" (another way of translating the Greek) is, therefore, precisely the demand of God to love our neighbor, as enunciated in Leviticus 19:18. So central is this command for James that much of the material in this letter can be read as a reflection on the implications of Leviticus 19 for the Christian life. Thus, the Christian is not to crush the poor by withholding wages (5:4; cf. Lev. 19:13) or, more subtly, by showing partiality in the judging of disputes (2:1-9; cf. Lev. 19:15). The Christian is not to swear (5:12; cf. Lev. 19:12), not to slander a brother (4:11; cf. Lev. 19:16), and not to bear a grudge (5:9; cf. Lev. 19:18).

Living faith in God, therefore, is to be articulated by response to the needs of others in love. It is not enough to avoid oppression and injustice; faith in God demands fidelity to the needy: "If a brother or sister is ill-clad and in lack of daily food, and one of you says to them, 'Go in peace, be warmed and filled,' without giving them the things needed for the body, what does it profit? So, faith by itself, if it has no works, is dead" (2:15-17). It will be noticed that James does not tell us that care for the needy emerges out of a program of social melioration. It is an articulation of faith in the one God.

James is therefore able to reiterate the classic statement of the Law and the Prophets for Christian faith: "Religion that is pure and undefiled before God and the Father is this: to visit orphans and widows in their affliction, and to keep oneself unstained from the world" (1:27). As James understands the term *world,* the two parts of the statement go together.

No ritual purity or separatism is intended here. Rather, the stance of faith in God means that the measure of human worth is not that given by the world, which is "false to the truth" (3:14), but that given by the one who "brought us forth by the word of truth that we should be a kind of first fruits of his creatures" (1:18). Only because this "word of truth" (the good news about and from God) has been "implanted" (1:21) in the heart of the believer, only because the Christian seeks life and worth in the one who "fathers-forth whose beauty is past change" (Hopkins), is he or she able with pure heart to "visit orphans and widows in their affliction" (1:27).

The Gospel

The "royal law" of Leviticus 19:18, which is so central to James's perception of faith's demands, is found on the lips of Jesus in Matthew 22:39 and Mark 12:31 in response to the question concerning the greatest commandment in the Law. To the demand of loving the Lord with all one's heart (Deut. 6:5), Jesus adds the command to love one's neighbor as oneself (Lev. 19:18). Rather, he does not *add* it, for it was in the Law all the time. But by placing these two commands in immediate juxtaposition (and the Gospel writers variously merge them) Jesus asks us to understand *each* in light of the *other*. This is one of the cases in which James and Paul seem to stand equally close to the teaching coming from Jesus, for Paul, too, says, "through love be servants of one another. For the whole law is fulfilled in one word, 'You shall love your neighbor as yourself'" (Gal. 5:13-14).

In Luke's Gospel, we find the same combination on the lips of a lawyer, who is testing Jesus by asking how he can inherit eternal life. When Jesus asks the man what he has discovered in the Scriptures, he responds, "You shall love the Lord your God with all your heart, and with all your soul, and with all your strength, and with all your mind; and your neighbor as yourself" (Luke 10:27). We notice that the two commands have been completely fused. Jesus, naturally, approves this answer. But the lawyer pushes the matter further: "desiring to justify himself," he asks another question, "And who is my neighbor?" (10:29).

It is necessary to recognize the implications of this question. The man wishes to "justify" himself, that is, he wishes to shape the commandment of God into a program capable of performance, so that at some point he can stop and rest, and say, "I have accomplished the commandment of God." For this to happen, it is necessary first to know the limits of the commandment; how far does it extend: "Who is my neighbor? Need I love my companion, my compatriot, the members of my intentional community?" Jesus responds with the story of the Samaritan who helped the man who had been beaten by thieves. By the mere telling of the story, he turns the lawyer's question completely around. After recounting the way in which the Samaritan, in contrast to the priest and Levite, had compassion for the robbed man, cared for him, and paid for his further care, Jesus asks, "Which of these three, do you think, proved *neighbor* to the man who fell among robbers?" (10:36). This is a dramatic and radical reversal. In the Gospel, fulfillment of the royal law is no longer (if it ever was) a matter of determining ahead of time who is a worthy recipient of my care, but rather of determining how I might, at every moment, discern how to show *myself* to be a neighbor to everyone I encounter. And this commandment has no end.

The story deserves closer attention, still. How did the Samaritan show himself to be a neighbor to the mugged man? It was certainly not by having that encounter on his agenda. He, as much as the priest and the Levite, had his own project for that day: they were all journeying somewhere. And each of them saw the man in distress. The priest and the Levite allowed their own projects to take precedence over the human need of the injured man and, by turning aside to continue their journey, refused to hear the implicit call of God to them in that specific situation. The Samaritan, no doubt, felt as threatened by the sight of the man as they had — probably, being an alien, even more. But seeing the situation in its truth, he saw his own project in relation to the human need of another. This human need *was* God's call to him, and he answered. He not only felt compassion (10:33) but expressed this compassion by his complete availability to the wounded man, where the man was; he literally had to step out of his own space into the place where the man lay hurting. He did what needed to be done, not because he had planned for this to happen, but because he could hear the voice of God in the man's cry. He did what had to be done, not in terms of his time and energy and plans and need to be needed, but in terms of the injured man's real needs. He "took care of him." To do this, he shared his possessions. He poured his own oil and wine into the man's wounds, sat the man on his own beast, and paid for his care with his own money (10:34-35). It goes without saying that this disposition of possessions expressed at every step his own availability to the man in time and energy and concern. Nor did his availability cease with referral. He tells the innkeeper, "Take care of him; and whatever more you spend, I will repay you when I come back" (10:35). There is an open-endedness to this caring, and an astonishing trust; he would repay whatever bill the man ran up.

Now we notice another thing. The Samaritan cannot abandon completely his own project; he cannot enter totally into the other man's life. It would not do for either. The Samaritan continues on his journey, picking up his personal project where he had left it to obey. But he will "come back and repay" however much is spent. In this story, the sharing of possessions articulates in an immediate and direct fashion the sharing of the self with the other. It is not surprising that patristic commentators saw in the Samaritan story an allegory about Jesus. In Luke's Gospel, Jesus concludes the story with the point to the Christian reader: "Go and do likewise" (10:37).

The unity between love for God and love for humans has never been more sharply or succinctly stated than in 1 John 4:19-21: "We love, because he first loved us. If any one says, 'I love God,' and hates his brother, he is a liar; for he who does not love his brother whom he has seen, cannot love God whom he has not seen. And this commandment we have from him, that he who loves God should love his brother also." The commandment received in the Johannine community is, once more, the royal law, found on the lips of Jesus in John 15:12, "This is my commandment, that you love one another as I have loved you."

The significance of John's statement lies not in its being a commandment so much as in its being the truth. We do not, after all, respond to God in isolation, or, except in the most extraordinary cases, in an unmediated fashion. John tells us in another place, "No one has ever seen God; the only Son, who is in the bosom of the Father, he has made him known" (John 1:18). And, in his first letter, "No man has ever seen God; if we love one another, God abides in us and his love is perfected in us" (1 John 4:12). The persons we meet in this world, among whom we dwell and with whom we live, these bear the stamp of the image of God (James 3:9); they are the icons through whom we discern the face of the Father. The way we respond to them is the way we respond to God. There is no division between authentic faith in God and genuine love of others. When we reach out to our brothers and sisters in genuine love and understanding, our reach extends our grasp and enters the space where God dwells as the ground of their and our existence. To love the neighbor, to show oneself a neighbor to another by love, is to obey God in faith. The way we love our neighbor reveals the structure of our faith in God, in the most concrete terms:

> By this we know love, that he laid down his life for us; and we ought to lay down our lives for the brethren. But if any one has the world's goods and sees his brother in need, yet closes his heart against him, how does God's love abide in him? Little children, let us love not in word or speech but in deed and in truth. (1 John 3:16-18)

It will be noted that at the very end of his letter, John gives us the alternative: "Little children, keep yourselves from idols" (1 John 5:21).

The Modes of Faith and Love

The same pattern that structures the response of obediential faith in God structures the response of love for our fellow humans. When we looked at the faith of Jesus, we found that his response to the call of the Father was mediated by the circumstances of his concrete existence, in particular by the needs of those who needed his care. I suggested that, insofar as Jesus was as fully human as us, he must have had a project of his own that he wished to fulfill — dreams, desires, visions that were close to his heart. What made his response to God authentic and saving faith was not the lack of such a self-project but his willingness to move beyond it into the freedom of God's will, a will he could not predict and could not control but only hearken to. I suggested as well that God's will for Jesus did not unfurl all at once like a blueprint but only revealed itself to him piecemeal, as it does to us, in the moment-by-moment structures of his life. For Jesus to be able to respond, he needed to be *attentive* to the Father's Word in the shape of the season. His faith was an obediential hearing of God in the needs of the world.

The same is true of the response of love. Indeed, just as God's fidelity and loving-kindness (Exod. 34:6) are but two terms for the same divine availability to creation, so are the faith and love of humans but two modes of the same response to the mystery of the Creator. To love our neighbor is to be creatively faithful to God; to show fidelity to our neighbor is to love the Lord with all our heart.

If this is so, then it follows that the same norm applies to love as to faith. The articulations of our love will be as diverse as the situations of life itself. Love is "patient and kind," it is true; love "does not insist on its own way," certainly; love "bears all things, believes all things, hopes all things, endures all things" (1 Cor. 13:4-7), to be sure; love is that gift of the Spirit by which we "bear one another's burdens, and so fulfil the law of Christ" (Gal. 6:2). But *how* we are to be loving in specific situations is not spelled out for us, nor could it ever be. Love requires the same faithful attentiveness, the same sharp hearing of God's truth in the complexity of the here and now, the same willingness to move out of fear and compulsion, as does the response of faith itself. The modes of being loving are not described beforehand in a program of action, but are defined moment by moment in creative fidelity to God's revelation of his truth in the shape of this time and place. As with the response of faith, so with the response of love — *discernment* is the link between attitude and action.

As the situations change, so must the response of love; this is not a question of "situation ethics"; it is a question of creative fidelity. The demands of love cannot be circumscribed by quantitative limits, nor can the tightness of our response be certified. We cannot know ahead of time whether the way we respond is appropriate to the truth of the moment, the real needs of the other, or the plan of God for the world and us. But we are called to seek the truth and must try to discern it in the tangle of our lives. Authentic love for another may demand a "no" when a "yes" would be easier; may require a holding back when a giving would be more attractive; may, in fact, call for us to continue our own project rather than be submerged in the project of another, even though that "self-abnegation" may appear more heroic and loving. The asceticism of the truth, the discipline of discernment, is difficult and demanding, all the more so because it yields not sweet certainty but only hope. Love of neighbor, like faith in God, cannot be programmed ahead of time or governed adequately by rule or rote. Part of God's call to us is for us to pay attention to our lives. Like faith, love does have a norm, but it is the norm not of a rule but of a person: "In this is love, not that we loved God but that he loved us and sent his Son to be the expiation of our sins. Beloved, if God so loved us, we also ought to love one another" (1 John 4:10-11).

The Ways of Sharing Possessions

If what I have said above about the way in which our response to God in faith and to our neighbor in love is mediated by the circumstances of our lives, so that we must be creatively faithful and attentive to our own lives to discern the call of God and the genuinely loving response at each moment, holds at all, and if, as I suggested in the first part of this book, possessions symbolize our self-disposition toward God and other people in the world, then it should follow that the ways of sharing possessions will be as diverse as the situations of life themselves.

The mandate of faith in God is clear: we must, in some fashion, share that which has been given to us by God as a gift. To refuse to share what we have is to act idolatrously. Not only is that mandate clear, but also the symbolic function of possessions; because we are somatic creatures, the way we dispose of possessions signals and affects our response to God and other people in this world. Because we have been freed from that fear which forces us to grasp things for our very lives, because we can perceive ourselves and others as equally naked and equally gifted in existence by God, because by the grace of Jesus Christ we have been empowered to respond with a yes to the dark mystery of God, we are free to share. The proper thanksgiving for a gift is to give. But (and this is an important "but"), the ways of sharing possessions are determined by the discernment of the Spirit that leads us in the path of obediential faith and service, a discernment of the circumstances of our calling, and the genuine needs of the moment. What is an appropriate mode of sharing in this circumstance may not be in that. The call by God to faith is also a call to maturity and responsibility.

The significance of the sharing of possessions, whether by once-for-all donation or by steady almsgiving or by a community of goods, lies not in the social arrangement but in the way in which the disposition of the property expresses our self-disposition toward God and the world. The clenched hand, the stance of holding and hoarding our possessions (no matter how small or large), manifests and makes real our closure against God and the world. The open hand, the sharing of possessions (no matter how small or large), reveals and makes actual our availability to God and the world.

The modes of self-aggrandizement that flow from idolatry and reveal themselves in the holding of possessions are diverse. We can think of the man building storage barns; Lot's wife wheeling around desperately in the field; a man so busy with a cow he cannot answer a Lord's invitation; a rich man holding a spear before his hall filled with booty, waiting for and dreading the arrival of one stronger than he (Luke 11:21-22). The modes are diverse, but the focus is the same: the self, sought and grasped as a possession. Likewise, the modes of sharing possessions are diverse. We can think of the disciples flinging down nets and running after a preacher they did not even know; of Martha and Mary, making space for the teaching in their hearts by making space for the master in their home; and of the first believers in Jerusalem, being so "one of heart and mind" that they shared all without discrimination. The modes are diverse, but the focus is the same: God's life, received as a gift.

In this connection, it is fitting, at last, to look directly at what Paul says concerning the Christian use of possessions. The first thing we notice is that in contrast to Luke or James, Paul gives little explicit attention to the use of possessions. The second thing we note is that Paul presents no social program within which the use of possessions figures. In particular, we find no trace in his writings of the existence of or his wish for a community of goods in his churches. This makes Luke's picture of the community of goods in the Jerusalem church even more isolated within the New Testament writings and helps us determine how we should regard that picture. More of that will be discussed in the next chapter. Paul's perceptions regarding possessions fit generally into his understanding of Christian existence as eschatologically conditioned and his understanding of his apostleship.

Paul exhorts the Roman church to contribute to the needs of the saints and to practice hospitality (Rom. 12:8, 13), but he gives no more attention to this within the paranesis of that letter than to the paying of taxes (Rom. 13:6-7). The only time Paul uses the Greek word for possessions is in 1 Corinthians 13:3, and there he is contrasting some heroic donation of possessions to genuine love: "If I give away all that I have, and if I deliver my body to be burned, but have not love, I gain nothing." A more distinctively Pauline touch is found in 1 Corinthians 7:30-31, where Paul says that one of the consequences of living in a period of eschatological tension is that "those who buy [should act] as though they had no goods, and those who deal with the world as though they had no dealings with it. For the form of this world is passing away." The point of this, of course, is not that Christians are to stop buying or selling, but that in doing so they should not allow the measure of this world to be their measure; they should have an eschatological detachment. Paul does not encourage his churches to withdraw from society and form closed, intentional communities. The Christian church is not an alternative social structure, but a way of living in freedom within the world. So, Paul explicitly rejects leaving society (see 1 Cor. 5:10), but urges his churches to reject the measurement that is the world's (see Rom. 12:1-2). Paul is obviously upset when some of his Thessalonian converts conclude from his teaching on the coming of the Lord and eschatological detachment that they are to withdraw from the profane pursuits of other people:

> Now we command you, brethren, in the name of our Lord Jesus Christ, that you keep away from any brother who is living in idleness and not in accord with the tradition that you received from us. For you yourselves know you ought to imitate us; we were not idle when we were with you, and did not eat any one's bread without paying, but with toil and labor we worked night and day, that we might not burden any of you. It was not because we have not that right, but to give you in our conduct an example to imitate. For even when we were with you, we gave you this command: If any one will not work, let him not eat. For we hear that some of you are living in idleness, mere busybodies, not doing any work. Now such persons we command and exhort in the Lord Jesus Christ to do their work in quietness and to earn their own living. (2 Thess. 3:6-12)

The picture we get of Paul from this passage accords very well with the picture in Acts of one who worked for a living and encouraged others to do so as well. There is no trace of an organized community of goods, here; indeed, Paul excludes the possibility even for himself. Even though he had the right to be supported by the church, he abdicated that right for the sake of the community in order to give them an example. Paul's statement of the apostolic right to be supported by communities fits what he says elsewhere (1 Cor. 9:4-14; Gal. 6:6) and what we find in the pastorals (see 1 Tim. 5:17-18). Although Paul intended not to exercise this right so as not to "put an obstacle in the way of the gospel of Christ" (1 Cor. 9:12; 2 Cor. 11:7-12), he saw the support of leaders by the church as a sort of material and spiritual exchange: "If we have sown spiritual good among you, is it too much if we reap your material benefits?" (1 Cor. 9:11). The only community Paul allowed to support him in his missionary work was the Philippian church, with whom he appears to have had a particularly close relationship: "no church entered into partnership with me in giving and receiving except you only" (Phil. 4:15). Because of that material support, Paul can speak of their "fellowship" (same Greek word as in "partnership," above) in the work of the gospel (Phil. 1:5) and in grace

(1:7). Even with this church, however, Paul is quick to assert his independence: "Not that I complain of want; for I have learned, in whatever state I am, to be content" (4:11). This notion of "contentment" is not far removed, really, from that of "eschatological detachment"; it means, in fact, freedom (see also 1 Tim. 6:6).

Because Paul speaks so sparingly about possessions elsewhere, the extended treatment he devotes to the collection for the church in Jerusalem is all the more impressive (see Gal. 2:10; 1 Cor. 16:1-4; 2 Cor. 8:1–9:15; Rom. 15:25-31). That this collection was of great importance to Paul cannot be doubted. Even before his agreement with the leaders in Jerusalem to "remember the poor," he had been eager to do so (Gal. 2:10). He deployed the resources of his fellow workers in the organization and carrying out of the collection (2 Cor. 8:16ff.; 9:3ff.). He was careful to avoid any misunderstanding over the nature of the collection (2 Cor. 8:19-21). When it had been gathered, he asked the Roman church to pray that his "service for Jerusalem may be acceptable to the saints" (Rom. 15:31). Paul attaches an almost sacramental value to the collection of money. He speaks of it as a "liturgy" (Rom. 15:27), and as a "service" (2 Cor. 8:4; 9:1).

Paul wanted, by means of this gift of money from the Gentile churches to the mother church of Jerusalem, to establish a "fellowship" between Gentile and Jewish Christians (Rom. 15:26; 2 Cor. 8:4). By this material sharing, in other words, he hoped at once to symbolize and effect a spiritual unity between Jewish and Gentile believers. Paul's language here comes remarkably close to that of Luke in Acts 2 and 4, and close as well to the language of Hellenistic philosophers when they spoke of friendship (as we'll see in the next chapter). His language comes even closer when he speaks about this gift establishing an "equality" between the churches (2 Cor. 8:14). Although Paul is speaking the language of social leveling, however, it is clear that the "equality" he has in mind is the reciprocity of care, a dialectic of service: "if the Gentiles have come to share in their spiritual blessings, they ought also to be of service to them in material blessings" (Rom. 15:27).

If we were to read such strong language as this in the light of Acts 2 and 4, we might suppose that Paul is here calling for a churchwide community of possessions, a binding together of all the churches on the basis of an economic equality. This, of course, he is not doing. Not only does he give no indication of such an ideal elsewhere in his letters, but these texts themselves make clear what sort of response Paul is asking from his churches. It is not an institutional community of goods. Rather, Paul seeks from individuals within communities a free-will offering (2 Cor. 8:3; 9:5), as each one is able to contribute (1 Cor. 16:2). Some of Paul's Macedonian churches were themselves quite poor and afflicted besides, but gave beyond their means in a "wealth of liberality" (2 Cor. 8:2). Paul is not, therefore, seeking to level off economic conditions but to stir his communities to an appropriate response to the needs of others. "It is acceptable according to what a man has, not according to what he has not. I do not mean that others should be eased and you burdened, but that as a matter of equality your abundance at the present time should supply their want, so that their abundance may supply your want, that there may be equality" (2 Cor. 8:12-14). Equality here is not the erasing of differences but the alternation of attentive care. The manner of giving, therefore, should not be by exaction (2 Cor. 9:5) but a response to the gift given them by God.

Thus, the motivation Paul gives his Corinthian congregation is not based on the ideals of friendship or egalitarianism, but on the gift of God. They are to give because God has given to them. They are able to give because they have first received. It is not only that "God loves a cheerful giver" (2 Cor. 9:7), or that God will sustain them in life and give them even greater prosperity when they give generously (2 Cor. 9:8-11). No, their gift, ultimately, must be based on the gift given to them: "For you know the grace of our Lord Jesus Christ, that though he was rich, yet for your sake he became poor, so that by his poverty you might become rich" (2 Cor. 8:9). In the light of this gift (in which, truly, the "body" symbolized the "spiritual" gift), their giving is an act of thanksgiving to God for what they have received (2 Cor. 9:12). Their service to the needs of the saints is an articulation of their "obedience in acknowledging the gospel of Christ" (2 Cor. 9:13). The Corinthians are called to discern both the gift they have been given and the needs of those suffering in poverty, and the obedience of faith will lead them to respond appropriately, enabling them to give of themselves even out of their poverty. Their response of faithful love is expressed and made real by the sharing of possessions. This material giving is simply another form of what Paul expresses at the end of his exhortation: "Thanks be to God for his inexpressible gift!" (2 Cor. 9:15).

Theology and Ideology

In reflecting on the mystery of human being and having in light of the mystery of faith, we have found that the two mysteries are inextricably connected and the biblical writings speak most explicitly about the points of intersection. The tradition of which we are a part, and which we affirm, recognizes that as bodily creatures human beings inevitably must "have" as well as "be" and that the ambiguity of "being and having" involves an ambiguity about our identity and worth. This recognition is of the first importance. Human "owning" is not itself a result of sin but the consequence of being a body. Humans, therefore, cannot become completely "dispossessed" without losing their identity.

The tradition recognizes as well that we are creatures who invariably center our lives on that which we perceive to be ultimate; we are so constructed. It also recognizes that, left to ourselves, our fear of nonbeing is so great that we tend to center our lives in some fashion on a power that is less than truly ultimate but that we can possess and thus ensure and control our own worth. In a word, we tend to be idolaters. This tradition recognizes the power of idolatry as the fundamental sin and the way it can organize our projects of existence as projects of self-aggrandizement, moving from fear into compulsion.

The tradition does not characterize possessions as good or evil in themselves. Things do not contaminate or sanctify. What humans have is good insofar as it is a part of God's creation and God's gift to humanity. The human project of owning, on the other hand, is good or bad insofar as it corresponds to the truth of the situation. When possessions are acknowledged as a gift from God and shared with others, "having" is the necessary condition for "giving." But when the project of having, or the things possessed become a false god, and close a human being to the call of the true God and the needs of other humans, then owning is a sign of sin. The enduring temptation of possessions is to allow them to function as a measure of human worth. This temptation is as real for spiritual as for material possessions. The problem lies not with the things possessed but with what they mean to the possessor.

The Scriptures do not present for our consideration or implementation any grand scheme for the proper disposition of possessions. There is no Christian economic structure to be found in the Bible, any more than there is a Christian political structure or educational system. The Bible does not tell us how to organize our lives together, and still less which things we should call private and which public. Nor does it propose a clear program of social change. It does not even present one way of sharing possessions as uniquely appropriate. A Christian social ethic must be forged (repeatedly, as in theology) within the tension established by two realities: the demands of faith in the one God who creates, sustains, and saves us and the concrete, changing structures of the world we encounter in every age.

This lack of a Utopian vision or specific social ethic may be regarded by some as a loss, but it is not. It is a blessing. If the scriptural witness on possessions could be reduced to an ideology, it would not be God's Word to the world, but humankind's. It is part of the task of theology to recognize that we are all, even as theologians, ideologues. As we seek to establish our own project of existence and resist the call to faith individually, so do we try continually to impose our perceptions of what the kingdom should be on the concrete circumstances of our life. But the Word of God stands in judgment on the theologian as ideologue, and says, "faith calls you to a country whose dimensions you do not know, of whose wealth you have no control, and of whose standards you know only enough to distort."

The theologian who reflects on possessions in this way knows that as Christians we are called to, and must struggle with, the age-old conditions of poverty and affluence, oppression and injustice, slavery and alienation, suffering and hunger; but as we struggle, we must not lose sight of the reality. What we are struggling with is not a series of problems, capable of resolution if only the proper structural analysis could be made, the proper people aligned, or the proper program forged. No, what we struggle with (within!) is the mystery of the human condition, rooted in ambiguity, scarred by sin, moved only with great reluctance, and never completely, toward faith.

If there is to be theological discourse about possessions, it must be marked by modesty before the mystery. We simply do not *know* how being and having interact within us. How, then, are we to know the shape the kingdom is to take or how to draw a blueprint for its construction? If this was not available to Jesus as a possession, it is not likely to be available to us.

Theological reflection on the mystery of human possessions does not lead immediately to a plan of action but to a *recollection* of who we are before God and, if it is truly theology, to conversion and praise. For theology to exercise its proper critical function within the community of faith, it should not only respect the mysterious dimensions of human existence, and not reduce them to problems, and the mysterious dimensions of God's Word, and not reduce it to an ideology; it should also recognize that there is a proper and inevitable tension between the mysterious and the problematic, between that which we can solve and that which we can only suffer. It should acknowledge that there is a complexity to the human structures of society that is not addressed directly by God's Word but that can be addressed by those who are equally attentive to that Word and the words spoken by this tangled world.

Theology can discover and contemplate this: the sharing of possessions is an essential articulation of our faith in God and of our love for our fellow humans. But how and in what fashion that sharing is to take place is not the task of theology but of the obedience of faith.

Comment

This chapter returns to reading Scripture with respect to what it says concerning the use of possessions, now informed by an analysis of Scripture from the theological perspective of faith and idolatry. That analysis yields the twofold principle that shapes this reexamination of Scripture: namely, the way we view God determines how we view other people, and the way we respond to other people is in fact the way we respond to God. These principles restate the basic conviction of covenant: Israel's fidelity and obedience to God is expressed by carrying out the covenantal qualities of loyalty and love in regard to other people. It is difficult to overstate the importance of the unity of the love of God and love of neighbor, and it is equally difficult to truly live by the conviction that the openness, generosity, and acceptance we display toward other humans is in fact how our obedience and faith toward God is expressed.

I experienced considerable delight in writing this chapter, because what I suspected to be the case turned out to be so: reading one scriptural witness after another, I found confirmed my suspicion that language about the use of possessions was intimately connected to language about covenantal loyalty and obedience. Faith in the one God is expressed on one side by the refusal to cheat or steal or oppress, and on the other side, by a variety of modes of sharing with others. Even in those parts of the wisdom tradition that saw prosperity as a result of covenantal loyalty are unanimous on two other points: first that such prosperity be righteous, disconnected from theft and injustice, and second that wealth be shared generously with others.

Looking back on this section of the book, I am reminded of how dense and pervasive is the attention given to doing justice with regard to possessions, in both testaments, and how perverse a distortion of a genuine scriptural sensibility it is when contemporary Christians obsess over the relatively little notice given to sexual prescriptions and completely ignore Scripture's constant preoccupation with the body language of possessions. In my judgment, Scripture regards the body language of possessions as the most direct and important expression of faith and idolatry. Glancing at the long chains of citations placed within parentheses as I make each point concerning the respective biblical witnesses, my greatest sense of failure is not having treated some of those passages with greater exegetical attention. But at least the data are there, and a diligent reader who pursues them will be rewarded with a fuller sense of the scriptural witness. And the brief readings I do provide of James, Luke, and 1 John provide at least a glimpse of how the New as well as the Old Testament speaks to this issue.

The chapter ends with what I still consider to be the essential point made by my argument. The task of theology is to understand and articulate how and why the disposition of possessions is a mandate and symbol of faith. But it is the task of faith's discernment to determine in specific circumstances how possessions are to be shared. Herein lies the freedom that is proper to the life of faith. The Spirit that works in believers as it worked in Jesus does not express itself in set and inflexible structures that suit our desire for good order and control, but rather expresses itself in flexible and creative responses to the real needs of others. Such freedom, such faith, is filled with risk and ambiguity, for we can never be certain, at any given moment, that our response truly does respond to others' needs rather than our distorted perceptions. But the risks of such freedom given by faith are gladly embraced by those who seek to live by the pattern of Jesus, whose entire existence demonstrated such extravagant and carefree sharing of God's wealth.

CHAPTER 4

Critical Observations on the Community of Goods and Almsgiving

I n the first three chapters of this book, I have suggested that the sharing of possessions is both a mandate and a symbol of Christian faith. I have defined faith as the obediential hearing of God's Word in the circumstances of worldly life and have contrasted it with the self-aggrandizement of idolatry. Furthermore, I have suggested that although the Bible witnesses clearly both to the necessity of sharing possessions (as a corollary of faith in one God) and to the symbolic importance of doing so (the signifying of our self-disposition by the way we dispose of possessions), it does not propose a program of action for implementation or even establish one mode of sharing as uniquely and eternally valid. This, I think, is appropriate to the mystery of human possessing. It is the task of obediential faith (by the discernment of the Spirit) to discover in the structures of the moment the proper mode of fulfilling the mandate. Placing the burden on the discernment of faith, rather than on an ideological function of theology, makes the matter more, not less, serious.

But to say that there are diverse modes of sharing does not mean that all are equally appropriate at every time. To say that it is faith's task to discern the proper mode for the moment does not suggest that this discernment can take place without theological reflection. And to say that theology must resist the temptation to become ideology does not mean that theology can avoid its task of criticizing every reduction of faith to ideology.

In this chapter, I will put some critical (even hard) questions to one manifestation of sharing, the ideal of community possessions, and put beside them some remarks on another, the ideal of almsgiving. The ideal of community goods has appeared in the history of Christianity repeatedly, has legitimated itself by appeal to the Bible, and is practiced today in one form or another by many Christians. At times, it has been seen as *the* ideal way of sharing possessions for Christians. It is badly in need of some sharp questions.

The theologian should not ask about the economic efficiency of the practice, but about its theological adequacy. Since every way of disposing possessions implies a vision not only of society but also of humanity and its relation to God, the following question concerning the anthropology and theology of community possessions needs to be asked: How consonant are these with the Christian perception of humanity before the one God? It may be possible, after all, to make frequent and repeated appeals to the Scriptures without the underlying rationale for a practice having much to do with the scriptural witness.

The question is made more urgent in this case because of the ambivalence of the historical evidence. Recent shocking instances of destructive and exploitive use of community possessions have been forceful reminders of the horrors of sixteenth-century Münster, and some individuals have even been moved to wonder whether the emergence of a Jim Jones or a John of Leiden represents a perversion of this practice or its logical realization. The same question is posed by the development of Marxist communism, which seems to be inevitably tied, where it is tried, to totalitarian rule. Is there some essential, or structural, connection between the benign forms of Christian communism found in monasteries or the Bruderhof movement and the malignant forms found in Guyana and Münster?

I think there is such a connection, and intend to show (very schematically) that the connection is found in the ideological strands woven into this practice before and after its baptism. I make no attempt to be fair here, only provocative. The reader will understand that more data form the background to this discussion than find their way into these pages. I cite only the ancient primary sources. My interest is in the structure of thought and practice rather than in the history of ideas.

The Community of Goods: Christian Ideal?

Although Christian forms of community possessions have usually looked (however lightly) to Acts 2:41-42 and 4:32-37 for their legitimation, it is clear that other influences have been at work in the shaping of the ideal. The passages in Acts themselves show the most obvious of these influences — the Greek ideal of friendship. By saying that the first Jerusalem believers were of "one heart and soul," Luke resonated the Hellenistic proverb, "friends are one soul"; and by saying that they "held all things in common," he echoed another traditional saying, "for friends all things are common." These statements were proverbial already in the time of Aristotle (384-322 BCE),[1] and the ideal they expressed played a significant, if not determining, role in the political writings of Plato (429-347 BCE),[2] to some extent those of Aristotle as well,[3] and the biographies of Pythagoras by Diogenes Laertius, Porphyry, and Iamblichus.[4] Already in this tradition, the disposition of possessions carried considerable symbolic weight.[5] But Acts is more than a passive tradent of this ideal. It stresses by repeating three times that the believers "laid [their possessions] at the apostles' feet" (4:35, 37; 5:2), and adds another dimension to the symbolism of goods held in common, making explicit a factor hitherto only latent in Greek Utopian thought: that the sharing of possessions tends to strengthen the hand of authority within the community.

Diogenes Laertius says that Pythagoras was the first to declare the ideal that "friends hold all things in common."[6] Whatever the origin of the saying, its impact on Greek thought was astonishing. Several factors appear to have contributed to this perception. The first is the typically acute observation of vice by the Greeks. All philosophers agreed that

1. Aristotle, *Nichomachean Ethics* 9.8.2. Compare Plato, *Republic* 449C, 449D, and 450C.

2. Preeminently in the *Republic* and the *Laws*.

3. Not only in the *Nichomachean Ethics*, but also in the *Politics*.

4. Although the critical problems concerning the connection between these late biographies (Diogenes Laertius, third century CE; Porphyry, late third century; Iamblichus, *ca.* 300 CE) and authentic traditions about the sixth-century BCE Pythagoras are real and vexed, it is possible to trace some of the material fairly far back, and it is clear that Plato himself was dependent on the Pythagorean tradition (cf. Iamblichus, *Life* 30.167). What is more to the point, the language about possessions in Plato and these writings is remarkably similar and shows a continuity of perception regarding friendship, unity, and equality, and the way they are symbolized by possessions.

5. This symbolism is particularly rich in Iamblichus, *Life of Pythagoras*, in which not only is the common life of the Pythagorean community expressed by property held in common (17.72), but ranks of initiation are symbolized by the increased pooling of resources (18.81) and expulsion of the misfit is expressed by the double gift of money that accompanies the excommunicate on his way (17.73).

6. Diogenes Laertius, *Life of Pythagoras* 8.10.

there was something drastically wrong in the way most people handled possessions. *Philarguria,* or love of money, is one of the three classic vices of Hellenistic moral philosophy.[7] They could see how a life devoted to the acquisition of money distorted a person's character and created dissension within society. They observed that the result of people making possessions their goal in life was bitter competition. So far, the analysis is accurate. But at this point, fantasy begins to take hold. We can almost follow the train of thought: Is there any relationship between humans in which there is not this fierce competition for possessions? Yes, in the relationship between friends. When people are friends, they do not draw hard and fast lines between what is "thine" and what is "mine." Why is this? Because friends are "one soul," that is, they have broken through the scandal of multiplicity at the spiritual level and operate as one; they have the same perceptions, desires, values, and outlooks.[8] But this kind of friendship, experience tells us, does not exist between slave and master, parent and child, rich man and poor; whenever there is difference, there is disputation. Friendship, therefore, can only truly exist between people who are in every respect "equal."[9]

Has there ever been a time, they seem to have asked, when this ideal of friendship, having everything for common use, coincided with the community at large? Yes, at the times of mythic beginnings, when there was no coinage or private property, when people lived as a family or tribe. People then dwelt together with everything in common; they were happy, and the social fabric was secure.[10] Now, this is a pleasant enough train of thought, but, even if it were true (and Aristotle himself worries endlessly about the ambiguity of the very term *equality*),[11] it would still be a big step from this reconstruction of the pleasant past to regarding the life of

7. See Dio Chrysostom, *Oration* 4.84; Iamblichus, *Life* 16.68; 17.77; Philostratus, *Life of Apollonius of Tyana* 1.34; Plato, *Republic* 421D; *Laws* 679C, 743C-D; Aristotle, *Politics* 1267B, 1271A, and everywhere in this literature.

8. Iamblichus relates the story of the friends Damon and Pythias as the supreme example of this, *Life* 33.235; see also 8.40. Aristotle, *Nichomachean Ethics* 9.4.5, says a friend is "another self" and, in the same context, speaks of friends as having but "one soul" (9.8.2, cf. 9.12.1). Compare Porphyry, *Life of Pythagoras* 33, and Plato, *Republic* 351D.

9. For "friendship is equality," see Aristotle, *Nichomachean Ethics* 8.5.5; 8.6.7; 8.7.3-4; 8.8.5; 9.8.2; Diogenes Laertius, *Life* 8.10; Plato, *Laws* 757A, 837A-B; Aristotle, *Politics* 1287B; Iamblichus, *Life* 20.162.

10. Even that non-Utopian rationalist, Aristotle, saw the family as a basic social unit that held all in common (*Politics* 1257A).

11. Aristotle, *Politics* 1282B.

friendship as the very stuff of societal relations at their best and trying to express this by the abolition of private property in the city-state.

Utopian thought almost always represents a return to the primitive. Thus, for Plato, the basis of the laws he proposes for the ideal city-state was the primitive communism that he supposed existed in early times.[12] For Porphyry and Iamblichus, the ideal of community possessions was most perfectly expressed when Pythagoras first founded the community at Croton.[13] For Luke, the time right after the bestowal of the Spirit on the Christians was the time when all goods were held in common. These authors not only saw the past as an ideal; they considered the recall of the past to serve as a model and an alternative to the present way of doing things. The ideal past could serve as a paradigm for the life of an intentional community (a philosophical school or church) or for the reform of the larger society (the city-state). So Plato declared himself to be sketching the ideal city-state as a possible paradigm.[14]

A further step is taken, however, when this Utopian ideal becomes a program of action; then it becomes ideology. Of the writings we have from the Greek tradition, Plato's *Laws* probably come closest to serving this kind of ideological purpose,[15] though even the "Lives" of Pythagoras appear to function as models for Pythagorean communities, actual or potential. The task of the Utopian as an ideologue is to structure society in such a fashion that the spiritual ideals of friendship, unity, and equality can be accomplished. If friends hold all things in common, including their material possessions, then this must be best for society as a whole. Clearly, the pursuit of private property has brought about only divisiveness, instability, and vice. By abolishing private property, it must be possible to secure unity, stability, and virtue. It will immediately be noticed that the structure carries an enormous load. Change the structure, it is thought, and you change the mind. This is, of course, testimony to the pervasive symbolic expressiveness of possessions. But it misses the point by placing the problem in the property rather than in the acquisitive human heart. Already, one senses, there is a certain spiritual violence here;

12. See Plato, *Laws* 679B, 684D, 744E, 745A.

13. Iamblichus, *Life* 6.29-30; Porphyry, *Life* 20.

14. Plato was conscious of the "paradigmatic" character of his proposals; see *Republic* 472C; *Laws* 744B, 746A-C.

15. It is difficult to know how seriously Plato intended his paradigm to be taken, but even within the literary setting of the *Laws,* the Athenian Stranger sets about to "found the state by a word" (702E).

the economic structure of the society is to achieve spiritual transformation. It is understood that the same measure that applies to friendship
applies here as well. The key to harmony is equality, and since possessions are a symbol of identity, making everyone's possessions equal will
establish justice in the state.[16]

Certain important and enduring aspects of this ideal of community
goods can now be located. First, the ideal is *unity.* In the philosophical
framework of Pythagoreanism and Platonism, unity is not only a moral
but a metaphysical consideration. Duality and multiplicity are scandal-
ous. The One is always ontologically superior to the Many. One of the
beauties of friendship is that it seems to break down the multiplicity and
make persons become "one soul." The Greeks, I think, took "one soul"
more seriously than we might. The unity (or "harmony") between friends
is closer to identity than to reciprocity.[17] Iamblichus sees the Pythagorean community, with its goods held in common, as participating in a
friendship "with all living things"[18] and as a friendship with the gods.[19]
The community of goods symbolizes and makes real the spiritual unity
of all being! Plato, in turn, extends this ideal to the city-state. He wants
citizens who will virtually "breathe together," so intense is their spiritual
unanimity.[20] It is axiomatic for him that the greater the unity of the city-
state, the better.[21] Plato says unequivocally that the strength of the city-
state lies in its being *one;* indeed, its capacity for expansion is limited by
its ability to remain not a multiplicity but a unity.[22] Within this understanding, a claim to be "other" is almost by definition a vice. When this
claim is symbolized by the statement "this is mine" regarding property, it
is divisive.[23] The individual is less important than the community; in
fact, the individual finds true identity by merging with the community
identity as much as possible.[24] It is not by accident that the doctrine of

16. Iamblichus, *Life* 30.167; Plato, *Laws* 684D, 744B, 757A, 837A.

17. Aristotle, *Nichomachean Ethics* 8.8.5.

18. Iamblichus, *Life* 16.69-70.

19. Iamblichus, *Life* 8.39; 10.53; 33.240.

20. Plato, *Laws* 708D.

21. Plato, *Laws* 739C-D.

22. See the development in *Republic* 343B to 443E. In the middle of this exposition
comes the key phrase, "for friends hold all things in common," 424A.

23. "That city is best ordered in which the greatest number of people use the expression 'mine' and 'not mine' of the same things in the same way," *Republic* 462C. Plato extends this to mean even the feeling of pain and pleasure!

24. Plato, *Republic* 462D-463E.

metempsychosis (with its minimal appreciation for individual human life) should flourish in this tradition. The symbolic function of possessions in this context is clear. When I claim to own something or hold something private, I resist merging with the whole and make a claim for individual significance. When I pool my possessions with those of the community, I signal the relinquishment of any individual claim or right within the community. Plato is quite clear on this. His aim is not the happiness of individuals within the city-state, but the happiness (justice) of the city-state as such.[25]

Such a preoccupation leads to the second characteristic of this ideal. A community of goods is particularly given to strong *social control*. Not only does the sharing or nonsharing of possessions symbolize who is and who is not a member of the community, but degrees of sharing function to symbolize progressive stages of entrance into the community.[26] Furthermore, community control over possessions means effective control over the persons who require those possessions to live. The withholding of basic possessions such as food is an efficient means of punishment and, therefore, of behavior modification. Excommunication from a community of goods can, in some circumstances, mean death.[27] Relinquishing the claim to self-determination by relinquishing control over possessions makes a person vulnerable to overt and covert manipulation by those who control the possessions. In this tradition, it is not surprising to find the control moving in the direction of uniformity. In Plato, we find some of the logical extensions of this ideology. Plato thinks there should be a community of wives and children as well as of property.[28] And since

25. Plato, *Republic* 420C. So strong is this dominance of the whole over the part, that Plato would desire each person who has received a portion of the land from the state still to regard it as the common property of the state, *Laws* 740A. In *Laws* 697B he speaks of the three "goods" of the state as being the soul, the body, and property.

26. This is found in virtually all intentional communities that practice community goods. See Iamblichus, *Life* 17.72; 18.81. Of all the manifestations of community possessions I have studied, that in Iamblichus is the most puzzling. Instead of confiscating the goods of one who leaves the community (the usual practice), the Pythagoreans are said to pay him double the amount with which he entered. Then they erect a tomb to him as though he were a dead man. See *Life* 17.73. The progressive donation of possessions accompanying progressive entrance is well witnessed by Qumran, 1QS 1:11 and 6:17-22.

27. As Josephus points out in reference to the Essenes in *The Jewish War* 2.143.

28. Plato, *Republic* 423E; 449C-50D; 457C-58C; *Laws* 739D. It will be noted that Plato did not hesitate to assign women and children to the category of possessions, in *Republic* 451C.

the purpose of this ideology is to bring about the perfect state, it is logical
to allow only certain kinds of people to breed and bear children; genetic
engineering is a comfortable corollary of the community of goods.[29]
Complementary to this, there is the thought control that bends the community to be "one soul." To say "This is mine" in reference to an idea is as
threatening to stability and unity as to say "This is mine" of a field or cake.
A substantial portion of Plato's thought, therefore, went into the question
of the education of children within the society so that the ideals of the
state could be implanted early.[30] Education here, of course, means simply
indoctrination, and the way to this is through rigid censorship.

One of the manifestations of social control is the erection of firm
boundaries between those inside the community and those without.
Here, again, the sharing of possessions serves to symbolize the reality.
Those who have their goods together are of "one mind" by definition. In
all these forms of community possessions, intercourse with outsiders is
avoided; mingling in the possessions of others is virtually a form of spiritual contamination.[31] In Plato, as always, the logic of this impulse is
carried through to an extreme: the ideal community will have its own
coinage, valueless outside the realm;[32] fomenters of sedition will be
sent abroad and their portion of land confiscated;[33] the ideal city will
not be located by the sea, for from there come all sorts of alien and
harmful influences.[34] Boundaries are necessary for the preservation of

29. Plato, *Republic* 456E. Plato carries this through rigidly in the *Republic,* reckoning
that since all children have the same parents, dissension would be eliminated; see
464E-466C.

30. Plato, *Republic* 424Aff.; *Laws* 788Aff.

31. Even the relatively mild separation of the Pythagorean school can at times be
sharply stated. The reason members of the community are not to associate with those
who have left is that it is not right to make "the goods of wisdom common" to one who has
not purified the soul; Iamblichus, *Life* 17.75. And, in fact, although it appears that Pythagoreans shared goods with each other, they refused to do so with outsiders, treating anyone
outside the fellowship as a stranger. As might be expected, this caused resentment (*Life*
35.257). Pythagoras told his followers that friends were to be treated as gods but others as
beasts (*Life* 25.259).

32. Plato, *Laws* 742A-B.

33. Plato, *Laws* 856D.

34. Plato, *Laws* 704E. The boundaries were especially well marked at Qumran. See 1QS
5:1-3; 9:8; 5:4-16; CD 13:4. The same caution regarding the "outside" is shown in the *Rule of
Benedict's* legislation on the reception of visitors (chap. 53) and monks returning to the monastery from a journey: "Nor let any one presume to tell another what he has seen or heard
outside the monastery, because this causes very great harm" (*Rule of Benedict,* chap. 67).

any community. This is obvious; but what is also clear is that the strict community of possessions tends to draw these boundaries with exceptional sharpness and rigidity while reinforcing them by mind-control within the borders.[35]

A third aspect of a community of goods, even of the "friendship" type, is the tendency toward an *authoritarian structure.* The question of authority arises as soon as there is a group too large for constant face-to-face interaction. The fluidity and casualness possible in the give-and-take regarding possessions among only two or three friends cannot obtain for any larger group. Some regulation is required. Now, here is where the ideology of friendship and the demands of structure conflict. If the possessions of a community are held in common, and everyone is thereby equal, then who shall be in charge of collecting and distributing possessions? Clearly, it cannot be everyone, for then we would be back with private possessions. Therefore, collection and distribution must be carried out by some constituted class or authority within the community.[36] How can this be determined? By popular election? No, for the masses cannot be trusted with so important a decision.[37] Ideally, the logical and qualified person will emerge. In the *Republic,* he is the philosopher king. In the *Laws,* when the Utopian fever was truly upon Plato, the man who should administer the laws is described as one who has himself observed them perfectly and shown no spark of individuality or disobedience. This one is best suited to carry out Plato's program.[38] It does not require much imagination to see how the central control of possessions will serve to strengthen the symbolic hand of authority and expe-

35. Plato is insistent that even the most private of acts must be legislated in the ideal state, *Laws* 780A.

36. In Iamblichus, *Life* 17.72-74, the initiates' goods are put in the charge of those called *Politikoi* or *Oikonomoi.* There is no evidence that these played any other authority role in the Pythagorean group. I have not yet sorted out all the functions of the "guardians" *(phylakai)* of the *Republic* 374Eff., or of the "law wardens" *(Nomophylakai)* of *the Laws* 752E, 754D, 755A. In the *Republic,* the guardian class is expected to observe the community of goods in the highest degree (416D-417B, 456B-458E), but it is not clear that they distribute goods within the state. In *Laws* 761E, Plato speaks of "land stewards" who distribute goods unjustly. The whole structure of authority in Plato's Utopia is muddled, at least to this reader.

37. Not only that, but the inevitable disputation about the allocation of possessions would threaten the "one soul" of the community. Remember that the structure here is supposed to ensure the spiritual, not the reverse.

38. Plato, *Laws* 715C.

dite the process of social and thought control.[39] We do not find all of this explicitly tied together in Plato, but the seeds are there. The first time, historically, that a community of possessions and a strictly authoritarian structure find each other is at Qumran.

Before moving to that development, it should be noted that one of the first criticisms of the community of goods remains one of the best. Aristotle placed his finger squarely on the essential deficiency in Plato's thought regarding possessions. He saw that the problem of human possessiveness would not go away with the structural equalization of property, for the problem lay not in property but in human desire.[40] The pooling of goods would not by itself effect a spiritual transformation.[41] Given the state of human nature, Plato's ideal could not be realized. Aristotle also saw that a community of goods inevitably demands a strong central authority to administer it. If all hold all in common, all will be equally neglectful. Without a strong sense of personal engagement with property, people are not going to have a sense of responsibility for it.[42] Above all, Aristotle attacked Plato's notion of unity.[43] He insisted that oneness in a society was not a matter of uniformity, but of plurality and reciprocity.[44] Equality is not susceptible to quantitative division but must be seen in terms of proportionality.[45] Rather than equalize all holdings in the city-state, Aristotle would rather work on the attitudes of people regarding wealth. As for the property itself, he would like it to be privately owned but shared in common by consent.[46] Aristotle is a realist and a master psychologist. Yet, he continues to think about these matters within the framework provided by Plato and the Pythagoreans. For Aristotle, too, friendship is the greatest good of the state[47] and the

---

39. It is somewhat strange that the philosophical school most renowned in the ancient world for the closeness of its communities and affectionate fellowship, the Epicureans, rejected the community of goods as an ideal. Diogenes Laertius, *Life of Epicurus* 10.11, tells us, "Epicurus did not think it right that their property should be held in common as required by the maxim of Pythagoras about the goods of friends. Such a practice in his opinion implied mistrust [*apistia*], and without confidence [*pistis*] there is no friendship."

40. Aristotle, *Politics* 1266B, 1267B.

41. Aristotle, *Politics* 1263B.

42. Aristotle, *Politics* 1261A-62B.

43. Aristotle, *Politics* 1263B.

44. Aristotle, *Politics* 1261A.

45. Aristotle, *Politics* 1282B, 1301-2A.

46. Aristotle, *Politics* 1263A, 1329B.

47. Aristotle, *Politics* 1262B; see *Nichomachean Ethics* 8.1.4.

motive for society.[48] Therefore, his discussion moves, as much as Plato's, within the range provided by the proverb "friends hold all things in common," and he sees this as the ideal form of relationship.[49] And, since "friendship implies likeness and equality,"[50] no matter how much he struggles with the modes of equality, he is nevertheless caught in the same web. The strength of this proverb is astonishing.

There is this paradoxical pattern to the historical forms of community possessions. Where it has been relatively harmless, in terms of structure and ideology, it has also been short-lived. A community that depends on the goodwill, friendship, and virtue of its members, or the expectation that with the abolition of property will also come the abolition of strife, quickly finds itself shattered on the rocks of clashing egos and the struggle for power. The failure to recognize that material possessions do not provide the only opportunity for human acquisitiveness, and that competition and self aggrandizement can take many forms, has spelled the end of many communes. On the other hand, those groups whose sharing of possessions has proved successful (by survival) have invariably survived by means of a strong ideological framework, massive boundaries between the inside and outside, a pervasive system of social control, and a total authority structure. Before moving to that "obedience" model of the community of goods, however, it is important to ask some questions even of this benign "friendship" model. The Christian who wishes to affirm a community of goods as the ideal way of sharing possessions must ask about the compatibility of the Pythagorean and Platonic notions of unity, equality, and friendship with belief in one creating God. Are Christians "one spirit" because they are friends or because they have been given the gift of the one Holy Spirit? Is their spiritual unity based on a metaphysical relationship to all being or on personal obedience to the call of God? Does the God who has given each of us "a new name . . . which no one knows except him who receives it" (Rev. 2:17) desire us to lose that name for the sake of a communal uniformity of expression and thought? We must ask whether the very *structure* of a community of goods itself impels a community to think of spiritual unity not in terms of the diverse gifts given by the will of God's Spirit (1 Cor. 12:4-11; Rom. 12:5-8; Eph. 4:4-13) but as the "one soul" of a metaphysical or psy-

48. Aristotle, *Politics* 1280B, 1295B.
49. Aristotle, *Politics* 1263A.
50. Aristotle, *Politics* 1287B.

chological monism. The tendency of this practice to wash away individual identity (and therefore individual responsibility), moreover, becomes more dangerous in the next stage on the way to the Christian community of goods — the placement of the practice within a highly reflective and effective authority structure.

This is what we find in the community of goods practiced by the Jewish sectarians at Qumran.[51] We see here no trace of the Hellenistic ideal of friendship as the motivating force behind the practice.[52] Instead, this self-conscious remnant of Israel[53] practiced a community of goods that functioned to define community limits (symbolizing the split of the sons of light from the sons of darkness),[54] ensured social control (by means of punishments concerning property and exclusion from the community of goods),[55] and established the authority of the priestly class within the sect (the possessions being controlled entirely by the priests and Levites).[56] The strongly dualistic ideology of the group, together with its self-perception of being a temple of holiness within Israel,[57] gave a symbolic significance to the sharing of goods; these were

51. Once again I am using only primary sources, recognizing that the complexity of issues regarding these matters is thereby not avoided but only bracketed. With the majority of scholars, I accept the identification of the Qumran community as a particularly rigid form of Essenism, a movement that seems to have been fairly widespread and appears in several social forms. The Damascus Document probably reflects a more complex form of Essenism than does 1QS.

52. There is something of this in the descriptions of the Essenes in Greek. In Josephus, *Jewish War* 2.123-27, mention is made of their community of goods, but although attention is given to the motivation of purity (2.129ff.) and to the authority structure (2.124, 134), Josephus alludes only briefly to the Essenes' mutual affection (2.120) and despising of wealth (2.122) as possible motivations for community goods. Philo's account of the Therapeutae in *The Contemplative Life* again speaks of contempt for wealth (14) and help given to relatives by leaving possessions behind (13-14), and that their sharing of goods leads to equality and therefore justice (18). The overriding motivation appears to have been the desire to pursue wisdom without the distraction of possessions (16). The same themes dominate the fragmentary *Hypothetica* 11:1, 4, 11, 16. Pliny the Elder's *Naturalis Historia* 5.15.73 adds nothing to this; the only motivation for being together he can see is a world-weariness *(vita fessos)*. Only in Philo's treatise, *Every Good Man Is Free* 77, 79, 84-85, does the familiar theme of friendship and equality emerge with any clarity regarding the Essenes.

53. 1QS 8:5ff.; CD 3:13ff.

54. 1QS 5:1-3, 14-16, 20; 7:24-25; 8:22-23; 9:8; CD 10:18-20; 12:6-7; 13:14-15; 20:7.

55. 1QS 6:24-25; 7:6; CD 14:20; 9:10-15.

56. 1QS 6:17-22; 5:1-3; 9:7.

57. 1QS 9:3-11.

the pure possessions of the pure community.[58] Mingling one's goods with those of the righteous meant that one was a member of the righteous community; but to mingle one's possessions with the sons of the pit was to become impure oneself and, therefore, outside the community of the pure.[59] At Qumran, therefore, the ideology of purity rather than that of friendship or justice formed the legitimation of the community of possessions. The Damascus document indicates a mode of collecting goods that looks very much like almsgiving but is actually directed toward the members of the community.[60] Alms could scarcely be given to those outside the group which defined itself as pure, for it is not possible to share the goods of the righteous with those who (by not being members of the group) are defined as reprobate.

Qumran illustrates the ideological adaptability of community goods. The Qumran sectarians referred to themselves frequently as "the poor,"[61] but there is no connection between this self-designation and the practice of community goods. Neither is there evidence for ascetical or philosophical motivation.[62] The ideology, rather, was a rigidly developed form of apocalypticism in which the world was neatly divided into the good (those in the group) and the evil (those outside the group).[63] When we observe the way in which the language about possessions functions within the community rule, for example, we can see that a certain strengthening of the ideology results precisely from the practice itself.[64] Seeing itself as the authentic Israel, for example, it is natural that the community should have a priestly leadership. But this authority structure is given considerable strengthening (practically and ideologically)

---

58. 1QS 9:6.

59. See 4QpH 8:8-12; 9:3-5; 12:3-10; 4QpPs37 2:9-10; cf. CD 4:15-18 together with CD 6:16 and 8:4f.; see also IQS 5:19-20.

60. CD 14:12f.

61. See 1QS 1:36; 2:32, 34; 3:25; 5:13, 14, 16, 18, 22; 14:3; 17:22; 1QM 11:9, 13; 13:14; 1QS 2:24; 3:8; 4:3; 5:3; 5:25; 11:1; CD 6:16, 21; 14:14.

62. The closest thing to a spiritual motivation for any use of possessions is found in 1QH 10:22-25, 29; 15:23. But these passages reflect typical wisdom motifs rather than an ascetical outlook.

63. The passages dealing with the poor of the land in the pesherim on Habakkuk and Psalm 37 could throw light on the possible historical roots of the community's ideology and practice of community possessions. See 4QpH 8:8-12; 12:3-10; 9:4-5; 4QpPs37 2:8-9; 3:10-11.

64. It is entirely possible that the greater degree of stringency both in practice and ideology in the 1QS may owe something to the pressure imposed by a total institution.

when the distribution of all possessions is placed in its hieratic hands. The priestly ideology, in turn, gives further motivation for the preservation of the practice. At Qumran, we can observe clearly the dialectic connection between a separatist mentality and the practice of community goods and the full flowering of that tendency toward central authority we observed already in Plato. The way is prepared for the way in which Acts weds the unity motif to that of authority.

Because the passages in Acts 2:41-42 and 4:32-37 have functioned as the explicit legitimation for so many Christian manifestations of community possessions, it is of critical importance to see precisely where the Acts passages stand in the development I have been tracing, and to decide exactly what the texts say and what they do not. What is Luke saying? First, it is clear that Luke is relying on the Hellenistic expressions for friendship when he says that the first believers had all in common and were of one mind and heart; but the source of this unity is the Holy Spirit.

Second, this sharing of possessions took place at the founding of the community, right after Pentecost. Subsequent outpourings of the Spirit (Acts 8:17; 10:44; 19:6) are not followed by descriptions of possessions being held in common. We recognize, then, that as did Plato, Porphyry, and Iamblichus, Luke is making a statement about "how things were in the primordial beginning."

Third, when Luke says that "there was none needy among them," he is making reference to Deuteronomy 15:4, which promised that when the laws of almsgiving were perfectly kept in the land there would be no more needy persons. In a literary fashion, therefore, Luke is implying that the first Christian community fulfilled both the Greek longing for perfect fellowship and the Jewish desire for a land without poverty.

Fourth, by having the disciples lay the proceeds from their sold property at the feet of the apostles, Luke is symbolizing the authoritative role the apostles played in the primitive Christian community and the recognition of this authority by those who first believed.

Fifth, these passages have a definite and particular role to play in the theological message of Luke-Acts as a whole. Luke wishes to show that the believing community represents the authentic and restored Israel and that, in contrast to the leaders of Judaism who refuse to recognize the prophetic authority of the apostles, the "people of God" acknowledge this authority. In short, what Luke intends is not to say something here about the way Christians are to dispose of their possessions always and everywhere but to say something about the nature of the church as a people, whose unity is given by the Spirit; about the apostles, whose once-for-all authority certifies its teaching; and about the exclusion from the people of those who do not recognize this unity and prophetic teaching as given by the Spirit of God and not by humans (Ananias and Sapphira). And all of this is symbolized by the disposition of possessions.

Sixth, as I pointed out in the first chapter of this book, the picture of the sharing of possessions drawn here by Luke can be seen as idealized because of the tension between it and the rest of his narrative and teaching. There is no reason to think that he expected every subsequent Christian community to practice a strict community of goods. Rather, the idealized picture stands as Utopian in the best sense — it presents an image from the past of a kind of spiritual sharing and unity against which later communities could measure themselves. Luke is not proposing this picture as a concrete example to be imitated, by structuring a life on the basis of community possessions. To read these passages in Acts as providing the ideological legitimation for such a structuring of the Christian community is to misread them.

But this is precisely the way in which the monastic tradition of the West has read these passages. The monks sought the origins of their cenobitic life in the primitive Jerusalem community and saw themselves as successors to the apostolic life.[65] The Acts passages appear everywhere in the monastic legislation as the legitimation for having common goods.[66] But now, the additional note introduced by Luke (they lay their possessions at the apostles' feet) takes on new significance. If the monastic community corresponds to the Jerusalem church, who corresponds to the apostles, at whose feet the possessions were laid? The abbot of the monastery, of course. Here, for the first time, we find an explicit scriptural and theological legitimation for the control of possessions by the leader of the community. The abbot holds the place of Christ in the monastic community as the apostles held the place of Christ in the primitive community.[67] Once more, we see the ideological flexibility of the practice of community possessions. If there is an ideology that perme-

65. John Cassian gives classic expression to the understanding that monks were the successors of the primitive Christian community in his *Institutes* 2.5 and *Conferences* 18.5.

66. For example, Augustine, *De Sancta Virginitate* 45; *De Opere Monachorum* 25; Athanasius, *De Vita Antonii* 2; Jerome, *Epistulae* 58:4; 130:14; *Regula Magistri* 82:20-21; 87:14f. I will be looking closely at the regulations in the *Rule of Benedict*, which cites the Acts passages referring to possessions in chaps. 33, 34, and 57.

67. *Rule of Benedict*, chap. 2.

ates, for example, the *Rule of Benedict,* it is obedience. Everything in the rule is structured by this virtue or outlook or ideology. It is stated clearly in the prologue: "We return to God by way of obedience from whom we have strayed by disobedience."[68] But the *Rule* is so structured that the obedience to God (to Christ in the high Christology of the period) is mediated entirely by obedience to his vicegerent, the abbot of the community.[69] The abbot's authority is absolute (with very few exceptions) and pervasive.[70] What is more striking is the way in which the prescriptions concerning the community possessions intersect exactly with the ideological framework of obedience to the abbot.[71] When called by the abbot, monks are to leave whatever they are doing and respond immediately, "for they do not even have their own bodies and souls at their own disposal."[72]

In the *Rule of Benedict,* as in the Qumran writings, there is no ideology of friendship, or even an ideal of spiritual unity, underlying the community of possessions. The whole monastic life is geared to the ideal of self-abnegation through obedience, which is specified as obedience to the spiritual leader. There is little left of the "obediential faith" and discernment I described earlier. Obedience to God has been brought completely within the compass of a written code and the will of another human be-

68. The following should also be looked at for the role of obedience in structuring the self-understanding of the monks: chap. 5 (on obedience: obedience is the first degree of humility); chap. 6 (on silence: the disciple is silent and listens, while the master speaks); chap. 7 (on humility: seven of the twelve rungs of humility have to do with obedience). The exhortatory chapters, 71 and 72, enjoin the monk to show obedience to all, but especially to the abbot.

69. "Let the abbot, since he is believed to hold the place of Christ, be called Lord and Abbot, not for any pretensions of his own, but for the honor and love of Christ," *Rule of Benedict,* chap. 63. "The obedience which is given to superiors is given to God," chap. 5. See also chaps. 2 and 71.

70. See, for example, chaps. 3, 8ff., 20, 21, 22, etc. It extends down to the measure of food (chap. 24) and the size of garments (chap. 55). The close of the chapter on the observance of Lent (49) sums it all up rather well: "everything, therefore, is to be done with the approval of the abbot."

71. Chapter 33 cites Acts 4:32, about holding all things in common, but leaves out any mention of the believers being "one heart and soul." Rather, the "abbot's leave" and the abbot's distribution of the goods focuses this passage. The receiving of gifts is totally dependent on the abbot's pleasure (chap. 54). Acts 4:35 is cited in chap. 55, "distribution was made to each according as he had need," but extends the exclusion of private property to the inspection of bed-clothing by the abbot.

72. *Rule of Benedict,* chap. 33.

ing, who is obeyed not because of his wisdom or virtue, but because the ideology identifies him as sacred authority.[73] In this context, in addition to the other functions it always has in a closed community (setting boundaries, effecting social control), the community of goods serves to strengthen by theological legitimation the hand of authority and accentuate the utter dependence of the individual monk on the abbot.[74]

Western monasticism has been the longest lived of all the forms of community possessions. This is partly due to its moderation. The *Rule* itself places the abbot under the rule, and these constitutional restraints have kept monasticism from being swallowed in the flames generated by erratic charismatic leaders.[75] Another important survival factor has been monasticism's decidedly unromantic view of human nature; it takes fully into account the continuing acquisitiveness of the human spirit.[76] The most important factor contributing to the longevity of this form of community possessions, however, may be its successful merging of ideology and practice. For the community of goods to flourish in a monastery, there *need* be no friendship, no palpable purity, and no great spirit of unity, though, of course, there frequently have been all of these. So long as the rule and abbot are obeyed, however, the community fulfills its ideological function. By placing the abbot at the center of the community of goods, and by giving theological legitimation for his control of the community's possessions, and by stressing that this spiritual leader must be obeyed in all circumstances, monasticism unwittingly provided the ideological bridge to the unharnessed exploitation in the name of the community of goods practiced by self-designated messiahs such as John of Leiden and Jim Jones.

I have already indicated in passing many of the critical judgments I would like to make on the practice of community possessions, but by way of summary, I want to advance the following points in as provocative a fashion as possible. (1) The scriptural basis for the community of possessions as the ideal way for Christians to share goods is slender, su-

---

73. "Cenobites, that is, those who live in monasteries, serving under a rule and an abbot," *Rule of Benedict*, chap. 1.

74. Chapters 58 and 59 deal with the donation of property to the monastery by those entering. A youth offered at the altar is to sign away his patrimony by oath, "and in this way let every opening be stopped, so that the boy may have no expectations whereby (God forbid) he might be deceived and ruined, as we have learned by experience" (chap. 59).

75. *Rule of Benedict*, chaps. 2, 3, and especially 64.

76. Notice especially the connection of murmuring to the distribution of goods!

perficial, selective, and suspect. (2) As an attempt to construct a way of life on the basis of a Utopian vision of humanity, rather than on the discernment of God's Word in the concrete circumstances of worldly life, the community of goods is ideologically rather than theologically based. (3) Insofar as the community of goods seeks to remedy the imbalances between human beings by divesting them of property, it is not only naïve but fails to recognize the inalienable quality of "having" as an aspect of somatic existence. (4) Insofar as it considers equality to have been achieved by the leveling of possessions, it continues (wrongly) to use possessions themselves as a measure of worth and identity. (5) Insofar as it has confidence that structural communism will do away with human self-aggrandizement, it fails to take seriously the power of sin and idolatry. (6) When the practice is structured by the ideology of friendship, it diminishes the significance of the individual human person and the individual call from God. (7) When the practice is structured by the ideology of obedience, it replaces the responsibility of the human person to dispose of himself or herself and possessions in response to God's call in the circumstances of life with the demands of a rule and leader. In this context, the subtlest form of possessiveness, namely "works-righteousness," can flourish because of the possibility of perfectly fulfilling the demands of both the rule and the spiritual leader. (8) In the obedience model and to some extent in the friendship model, the community of possessions fosters an unhealthy degree of social control and, in many cases, of thought control. (9) A strict community of possessions tends toward spiritual solipsism. The practice supports those within the community, but there is no need to turn to the needs of those outside, for possessions are already being perfectly shared. Not only that, but where there is nothing an individual can dispose of there is nothing that can be given to others. (10) The practice of a community of goods, particularly in the obedience model, encourages spiritual immaturity, irresponsibility, and alienation. When the proper response in every instance is indicated by the rule or the will of a superior, the individual community member is encouraged to abdicate that discernment of the spirit which is the necessary corollary to the obedience of faith.

Not all of these critical comments may be valid. If any of them are, it indicates the need for theology to study more carefully the whole issue of the sharing of possessions. On the basis of my own understanding of the matter, I consider it past time to renounce our long romantic attachment to the community of possessions and to look more deeply into that part of our tradition which has flourished in Judaism to our own day but which is equally part of our Christian heritage. I speak of almsgiving, not only as an act of individual and occasional piety, but as a response of the believing community to the needy of our world.

Almsgiving: An Overlooked Option?

Although the writings of Philo and Josephus on the Essenes, the Qumran writings themselves, and the writings of Paul and Luke on the use of possessions can all be considered "Jewish" writings in the broad sense, it is remarkable to note how little impact the Hellenistic notions concerning friendship and the sharing of possessions had on those broad traditions we have come to call, with careful qualification, "normative" Judaism. In none of the properly rabbinic sources do we find the community of possessions even mentioned as an ideal.[77] Indeed, there may be in one place or another, though in very veiled form, a polemic against the sharing of possessions in this way.[78] Nowhere in this tradition do we find a Utopian scheme for the reshaping of society. What we find instead is the sedulous study of the demands of God's Word. The first thing, then, that should recommend this tradition to our consideration is the fact that it springs from the same understanding of God and of the world which we share as Christians. It is not a way of dealing with possessions that derives from Utopian ideology but one that derives from the application of the mandate to diverse circumstances.

The classic halakic Midrashim on the Laws, the *Mekhilta,* the *Sipra,* and the *Sipre,* all devote careful attention to the legislation concerning the care of the poor (especially the sojourner, orphan, and widow) in the Pentateuch. To the casual reader, these commentaries may appear as ceaseless casuistry. They are not. They show the soberest respect both for the complexity of ever-changing human circumstances and the continuing validity and awesomeness of God's mandate. The scriptural text

77. The earliest writings on the Pharisaic *Haburah* contain nothing about the sharing of possessions (see M. Demai 2, Tos. Demai 2, and bT Bekoroth 30a-31a), nor does the Mishnah Tractate *Erubin.*

78. The *Pirke Aboth* 5:10 characterizes one who says "what is mine is thine and what is thine is mine" as an *am-ha-aretz,* and in the late *Midrash Rabbah on Koheleth* 1:8, there is a confusing story that seems to associate the common purse of the *minim* (Christians?) with sexual immorality. But these references are vague and difficult to construe.

is consistently interpreted in such fashion as to give maximum benefit to the poor.[79] At the same time, the legitimate rights of property owners are scrupulously protected.[80]

The command to help the poor and needy in Deuteronomy 15:7-11 is interpreted by the *Sipre* with seriousness. Failure to help one in need is tantamount to throwing off the yoke of heaven; it is, indeed, the same as idolatry.[81] This Midrash shows a remarkable sensitivity to the needs of the poor. The scriptural phrase "sufficient for his need" (Deut. 15:8) is taken to mean that a person should be helped appropriately to his or her need — even a horse or slave could be given to one who had been used to such possessions.[82] Above all, attention is to be paid to the particular need of the poor person. Here, it is not a question of "making equal" but of caring. Even if the poor person needs to be handfed, this should be done.[83]

If the halakic Midrashim attend to the exigencies of the Law, the haggadic Midrashim give us the spirit of the tradition regarding poverty and the sharing of possessions. There is a sense in some of these haggadic reflections that both wealth and poverty come as gifts and testings from God. The rich person is tested to see if the poor are helped. The poor person is tested to see if affliction can be borne without complaint. Both will be rewarded if they pass the test. The poor person will receive a double portion in the life to come. The rich person will be delivered from hell if alms have been given to the poor; if not, the rich person will perish with his or her wealth. In fact, there can be no predicting how long one will stay wealthy or poor in this life, for riches and poverty are like a wheel, now favoring this one, now that.[84]

---

79. For example, Tractate Kaspa of the *Mekhilta* of R. Ishmael on Exodus 22:24-26 establishes that the conditional "if you lend money to any of my people" is one of the three exceptions in all of Torah to the principle that every "if" in Torah refers to a voluntary act. Lending to the poor, therefore, is mandatory.

80. The discussion of *Sipra* on Leviticus 19:9-10, for example, addresses the responsibility of the landowner to leave a "corner" (Peah) for gleaning by the poor. The Midrash seeks to establish what constitutes a corner. This may seem silly, but if a stream crosses a man's field, does he then have twice the corners (that is, two fields) that must be left fallow? Keeping on this way, he could run out of land.

81. *Sipre on Deuteronomy* 176:1-2, 4-6.

82. *Sipre* 175:12-14.

83. *Sipre* 177:5-7.

84. The previous paragraph in the text is something of a paraphrase of the homily on Koheleth 5:12 in Tractate Mishpatim 31ff. of the *Exodus Rabbah*.

The image of the wheel for picturing the alternation of wealth and poverty was not infrequent in the ancient world, but in this tradition it is not the blind "wheel of fate" that disposes,[85] but the will of the one who "makes rich and makes poor, who gives life and strikes dead." The point that the land was in the hands of the Lord, and that wealth or poverty were gifts and tests from him, gives us some insight into this tradition's resistance to a community of possessions. To equalize the property of all would not only challenge God's disposition of the world but would also make impossible the fulfillment of the command to give alms. We read,

> David said, "Lord of the Universe, make Thy world evenly balanced, as it says, 'Let the world be made equal before God'" (Ps. 61:8). God replied, "If I balance my world, then 'love and truth, who will practice them?'"[86]

Passages like these seem to imply that it is precisely the God-given imbalance of the world's fortunes which provides the opportunity to practice charity, which is conceived of as imitating God's own concern for the poor and outcast.

The suffering involved in poverty is not minimized. "There is nothing in the world more grievous than poverty — the most grievous of all sufferings."[87] The one who relieves this suffering by the giving of alms has, therefore, done a very great thing. "He who lends without interest is regarded by God as if he had fulfilled all the commandments."[88] The Midrashim, in fact, make some bold statements regarding the giving of alms to the poor. By an involved and daring collation of texts, commenting on Proverbs 19:17, "he that is gracious to the poor lendeth to the Lord" (a bold enough statement already!), R. Eleazar manages to suggest that the Lord becomes the servant of the one who lends to the poor, for "the borrower is servant to the lender" (Prov. 22:7).[89]

It is abundantly clear from the Midrashim that, as the agricultural laws of the Pentateuch became inoperable, the practice of almsgiving became the ideal, even the only way of redressing the plight of the poor

---

85. *Exodus Rabbah*, Mishpatim 31.3. See also *Ruth Rabbah* 5.9; *Leviticus Rabbah* 34.3; bT Shabbath 151b.

86. *Exodus Rabbah*, Mishpatim 31.5.

87. *Exodus Rabbah*, Mishpatim 31.12.

88. *Exodus Rabbah*, Mishpatim 31.13.

89. *Leviticus Rabbah*, Behar 34.2.

in Israel. References could be multiplied without end to show the centrality of almsgiving in the tradition. The following are only a few: "If a man busies himself in the study of Torah and in acts of charity . . . all his sins are forgiven him."[90] R. Nathan said, "The Holy One, blessed be He, says, if a man occupies himself with the study of Torah and with works of charity and prays for the congregation, I account it to him as if he had redeemed me and my children from among the nations of the world."[91] Charity delivers the soul from death and Gehinnom.[92] The practice of charity is one of the things for which a person enjoys the fruits in this world while the principal awaits him or her in the world to come.[93] Finally, Simon the Just said, "On three things the Age stands, on the Torah, on the Temple service, and on acts of piety (almsgiving)."[94]

The aspect of this tradition that most deserves our attention, however, is the way in which this virtue of almsgiving could be organized into a community practice of charity without losing its sensitivity to the individual needs of poor people and without being erected into a program of social reform on Utopian principles, among them a view of humanity incompatible with belief in the one creating and saving God.

As historical situations changed, so did the ways of providing organized help to the poor and disadvantaged. Deuteronomy 14:28-29 already spoke of collecting the tithes of every third year and storing them for the sojourner, fatherless, and widowed. While the temple stood, there appears to have been a special chamber where donations could be made for the poor and from which the poor could draw what they needed anonymously.[95] Whether this "chamber of Secrets" was an actual institution or only a reading back to temple times of a preoccupation of a later generation, by the time the temple was destroyed the dominant mode of caring for the poor in Judaism was the charity collection. Already in the Mishnaic period, this seems to have consisted of both short-range help (the pauper's dish) and long-range aid (the poor fund).[96] The charity collection can therefore be dated as a standing tra-

---

90. bT Berakoth 5b.

91. bT Berakoth 8a.

92. bT Shabbath 156b; Rosh Hashanah 16b; Gittin 7a, b.

93. M. Peah 1:1.

94. Pirke Aboth 1:2; on the greatness of charity, see also bT Sukkah 49b.

95. For legislation (possibly idealized) concerning the shekel temple tax and the care for the poor, see M. Shekalim 2:5; 4:3; 5:2; 5:6.

96. M. Peah 8:7.

dition already before the third century, and at that time it involved a regular collection and set officials.[97]

The same sensitivity in the care of the poor is found in these Mishnaic texts dealing with the charity collection. Human dignity must be respected even, or especially, in the poor. The various needs of the poor continue to be recognized. In the Mishnaic Tractate Pesachim, we read, "On the eve of the Passover, from about the time of the evening offering, a man must eat naught till the nightfall. Even the poorest in Israel must not eat unless he sits down to table, and they must give him not less than four cups of wine, even if it is from the 'Pauper's dish.'"[98] Poverty, in other words, shall not prevent a person from sharing in the dignity and freedom of the people in the celebration of the Passover. Again we read, "If an orphan was given in marriage, she shall be assigned not less than fifty zuz; if there was more in the poor fund, they should provide for her according to the honor due her."[99] Neither shall poverty exclude the poor from the joy of marriage in honor.

The Babylonian Talmud, especially in the Seder Nezikin, contains much material about the charity collection. Only a few points need be made here. The opinions of the rabbis concerning such pertinent questions as the amount to be given in charity by an individual are discussed.[100] The amount seems to have been determined largely by the degree of wealth one enjoyed. The rich could give more,[101] but the charity collectors were allowed to accept only small amounts from housewives. Since charity was a commandment that must be fulfilled, however, it was in some measure incumbent on all.[102] Thus we find this remarkable statement: "If a man sees that his livelihood is barely sufficient for him, he should give charity from it . . . Mar Zutra said, even a poor man who himself subsists on charity should give charity."[103] The heroic charity of men like Benjamin the Righteous who, himself a charity collector, gave a widow money out of his own pocket when the poor fund was empty, was praised.[104] On the other hand, ostentatious giving

97. M. Demai 3:1; M. Peah 5:4; Pirke Aboth 5:9.
98. M. Pesachim 10:1.
99. M. Kethuboth 6:5.
100. bT Baba Bathra 9a.
101. bT Baba Bathra 8b.
102. bT Baba Bathra 9a.
103. bT Gittin 7a.
104. bT Baba Bathra 11a.

was frowned on.[105] Certain limits to liberality were set,[106] and there was always a sense in which the giving of alms was properly an anonymous act.[107]

The Talmudic discussions devote considerable attention to the collecting of alms and to their distribution.[108] The issue of whether those who seek help are always really needy, or are sometimes imposters, must be faced.[109] The age-old difficulty of the door-to-door beggar is treated. After some debate, the conclusion is, "we do not listen to his request for a large gift, but we do listen to his request for a small gift."[110]

The Mishnah and Talmud try to ensure that men of probity and learning handle the charity collection, so that no scandal might arise.[111] Far from being resented, the charity collectors were esteemed, for they enabled people to fulfill God's command.[112] In some holy communities, such as that of R. Eliezer b. Birkah, this esteem and enthusiasm could be hazardous. "Whenever the collectors of charity caught sight of R. Eliezer b. Birkah, they would hide themselves from him, because he was in the habit of giving away to them all that he had."[113] As serious as the obligation of the collectors was, the burden placed on the distributors of charity was even greater. R. Jose said, "May my lot be with those who collect charity, but not with those who distribute charity."[114]

The urgency of caring for the people is indicated by the exception made to the general Sabbath obligation in allowing charity grants to be made on the Sabbath.[115] Raba said, "For charity offerings, one becomes liable at once. What is the reason? Because the poor are waiting."[116] And R. Eleazar said in the name of R. Isaac, "If on a fast day the distribution of alms is postponed overnight, it is as though blood were shed."[117]

105. bT Kethuboth 66b; Yebamoth 78b.

106. bT Kethuboth 50a.

107. bT Mo'ed Katan 16b.

108. bT Megillah 27a; Baba Bathra 8a-b; Rosh Hashanah 4a-5b.

109. bT Baba Bathra 9a; M. Peah 8:9.

110. bT Baba Bathra 9a.

111. M. Shekalim 5:2; bT Abodah Zarah 17b; Baba Bathra 8b.

112. bT Baba Bathra 8b.

113. bT Ta'anith 24a.

114. bT Shabbath 118b. See also bT Baba Kamma 93a for the complexities involved in handling the fund.

115. bT Shabbath 150a.

116. bt Rosh Hashanah 6a.

117. bT Sanhedrin 35a.

The contrast between this part of our tradition and the community of goods could not be sharper. Perhaps we could criticize the ideal of almsgiving for leading to a privatism or a quietism in the face of injustice. But in Judaism, this has never been the case. It is precisely the need to obey God's command to share the blessings of the earth with those without that has impelled such creativity in social action and such diversity in the organized forms for allowing alms to reach the poor. No people has been less privatistic or quietistic in the face of suffering of every kind, not the least of poverty. And in contrast to the ideology of community possessions, this way of fulfilling the mandate allows the structures of society to be treated as they should be, as profane but worthy works of human hands, and not the kingdom of God on earth. This tradition moves directly out of faith in the one creating and redeeming God. It is not here, as in the case of community possessions, an ideal picture of humanity that generates a program of societal reform, but the needs of God's creatures that call for care. It is not an ideology that leads to the exaltation of conformity, but the command of God that leads to self-sacrifice. It is not the human project that is advanced, but the obedience of faith that is articulated.

Conclusion

By questioning the theological adequacy of community possessions, and by praising the theological roots of almsgiving, I am by no means suggesting that one replace the other as a unique form of sharing possessions. That would run contrary to the whole point of this book. I have tried to show that the Scriptures, read as normative and not simply descriptive, challenge us to express our faith in God by sharing our possessions. Such sharing, indeed, is a mandate of faith, for clinging to what one has is incompatible with faith in God and an expression of idolatry. But the shape of the mandate, I have also suggested, is as diverse as life's circumstances and requires not an ideology but hard thinking about the inevitable symbolic shape of our lives.

I have tried, both in the introduction and in the second chapter, to share some of the thinking I have done on the symbolic nature of possessing. I do not suppose that I have thereby resolved the ambiguities or diminished the mystery of being and having. The point of its being a mystery is that it cannot be reduced to a problem; and certainly not one soluble in a little book.

Therefore, the point of this book has been to begin thinking about the mystery in a concrete and fundamental fashion. We cannot presume to know the shape even of our bodies, much less the shape of God's kingdom. And although dialecticians of various stripes urge us to revolution, I hold that a bit of despised contemplation is not a bad preparation. What distresses us the most about programs for the alleviation of poverty or the equalization of society is that so little thought seems to lie behind them.

Precisely this lack of critical thought concerning community goods has complicated the issue. One of the reasons the Jewish ideal of almsgiving (doing justice) recommends itself to our meditation and implementation, beyond the fact that it is communal without being communistic, beyond the fact that it deals with humans in concrete rather than ideal terms, is the simple fact that it is rooted in God's commanding Word and has been subject to the most critical and searching reflection for thousands of years. Christians need only pay attention.

Epilogue

M uch like Jesus' dictum concerning the poor — that they "will always be with you" (John 12:8) — the mystery of human having and
being, and the complex issue of relating this mystery to the diverse witnesses in Scripture, remains always open to investigation. I do not pre-
tend to have solved everything in this short book. I only wanted to stimulate a certain way of thinking.

Over the past thirty years, I have continued to think, speak, and
write on the topic of faith and the faithful use of possessions. I made
shorter and longer presentations to local congregations,[1] others to
ecclesial and political associations,[2] and still others to a range of academic audiences.[3] My further thoughts also found expression in scholarly and popular articles,[4] as well as in two chapters of books devoted to

1. Such as the Decatur Church of Christ in 1985 and 1992, the Plymouth Congrega-
tional Church of Fort Wayne, Indiana, in 2007, Saint Peter's Catholic Church in Charlotte,
North Carolina, in 2005, and the Church of the Holy Spirit in Atlanta, Georgia, in 2009.

2. For example, the National Stewardship Council of the United Church of Christ in
Connecticut (1983), the Continuing Education Committee of the Northeast United Church
of Christ in Pennsylvania (1985), the National Association of Endowed Presbyterian
Churches in Washington, DC (1992), and the Conference on the Church and the Environment in South Carolina (2003).

3. The Lancaster Theological Seminary (1997), the Aquinas Lecture in Social Justice
at Emory University (2006), the Lake Lecture at the Center for Philanthropy at Indiana
University and Purdue University in Indianapolis (2006), at the City Seminary of New York
(2007), at Loyola University in Chicago (2008), and at Northwest Nazarene University
(2008).

4. E.g., "James 3:13–4:10 and the *topos* PERI PHTHONOU," *Novum Testamentum* 25
(1983): 327-47; "Friendship with the World and Friendship with God: A Study of Disciple-

other topics.[5] As a way of keeping up with the thinking of others, I have also reviewed a number of books devoted in one way or another to the subject.

In this epilogue, I update my earlier work in three ways. First, I briefly review some of the work done by others, seeking thereby to provide readers with a sense of which contributions are worthwhile, and how *Sharing Possessions* remains distinctive within the flow of scholarship. Next, I respond to some of the criticisms of the first edition by reviewers. Even when I do not agree with the criticisms, I think it important to respond to what some readers (rightly or not) saw as the implications of my effort. Everything is to be gained by seeking greater clarity. Finally, I touch on a number of themes that are perfectly compatible with my earlier argument — indeed, largely arise out of it — but were not developed in the first edition: hospitality, stewardship, Sabbath, and discernment.

Other Contributions

In this edition of *Sharing Possessions*, I have kept intact the list of "Suggestions for Further Reading" that I included in my earlier effort. All of these resources retain their value. The only comment I would add now is to encourage readers even more urgently to acquaint themselves with the powerful way of thinking about the mystery of human existence found in the writings of Gabriel Marcel. If readers find my approach in this book valuable, they will find even richer resources in this great philosopher.[6]

---

ship in James," in *Discipleship in the New Testament*, ed. F. Segovia (Philadelphia: Fortress Press, 1985), pp. 166-83; "The Bible and the Poor," *Biblical Literacy Today* 3 (1989): 8-9; "Wealth and Property in the New Testament," *Priests and People* 12 (1998): 181-84; "Sacrifice Is the Body-Language of Love," *Priests and People* 16 (2002): 87-91; "The Material Expression of Friendship in the New Testament," *Interpretation* 58 (2004): 158-71; "Caring for the Earth: Why Environmentalism Needs Theology," *Commonweal* 132, no. 13 (2005): 16-20.

5. See "Faith Embodied: Possessions and Power," in *Faith's Freedom: A Classic Spirituality for Contemporary Christians* (Minneapolis: Fortress Press, 1990), pp. 114-30, and "Stewardship: The Sharing of Possessions by the Church," in *Scripture and Discernment: Decision Making in the Church* (Nashville: Abingdon Press, 1996), pp. 148-51.

6. I listed Marcel's *Creative Fidelity* because in many ways it is the most accessible of his works. Readers are encouraged to look into such works as *Being and Having*, trans. K. Farrer (London: Dacre, 1949); *Homo Viator: Introduction to a Metaphysics of Hope*, trans. E. Craufurd (Chicago: H. Regnery, 1951), and *The Mystery of Being*, trans. R. Hague (London: Havrill Press, 1949).

The first version of the book appeared during a period when the issues it addresses were engaged — and continued to be engaged — by a variety of other publications. Increased attention was given to the social context of earliest Christianity, including the social status and wealth of Christians. Wayne Meeks's *The First Urban Christians* built on earlier scholarship to suggest that Paul's readers were mostly in the middle range of the stratified Roman world,[7] and although that position has been challenged,[8] it remains influential.[9] The point of such study is to gain leverage on the New Testament statements concerning the use of possessions. Yet the reconstruction of the specific economic situation in Palestine,[10] as in the Roman Empire as a whole,[11] is extraordinarily difficult, and many of the efforts to interpret the theme of possessions by exploiting such a reconstruction — not to mention by appeal to a historical reconstruction of Jesus — are problematic.[12] Somewhat more helpful are

7. W. A. Meeks, *The First Urban Christians: The Social World of the Apostle Paul* (New Haven: Yale University Press, 1983).

8. J. Meggitt, *Paul, Poverty and Survival* (Edinburgh: T. & T. Clark, 1998); see also S. Friesen, "Injustice or God's Will? Christian Explanations of Poverty," in *Wealth and Poverty in Early Church and Society,* ed. S. Holman, Holy Cross Studies in Patristic Theology and History (Grand Rapids: Baker Academic, 2008), pp. 17-36.

9. P. Harland, *Associations, Synagogues, and Congregations: Claiming a Place in Ancient Mediterranean Society* (Minneapolis: Fortress Press, 2003).

10. For some of the issues, see S. Freyne, *Galilee, from Alexander the Great to Hadrian 323 B.C.E. to 135 C.E.: A Study of Second-Temple Judaism* (Notre Dame: University of Notre Dame Press, 1980); R. A. Horsley, *Archaeology, History and Society in Galilee: The Social Context of Jesus and the Rabbis* (Valley Forge, PA: Trinity Press International, 1996); S. Safrai, *The Economy of Roman Palestine* (New York: Routledge, 1994); J. Pastor, *Land and Economy in Ancient Palestine* (London: Routledge, 1997).

11. See especially the insightful essays in M. Atkins and R. Osborne, eds., *Poverty in the Roman World* (Cambridge: Cambridge University Press, 2006).

12. K. E. Bailey, *Poet and Peasant,* and *Through Peasant Eyes: A Literary Cultural Approach to the Parables of Jesus* (Grand Rapids: Eerdmans, 1983), and W. R. Herzog, *Parables as Subversive Speech: Jesus as Pedagogue of the Oppressed* (Louisville: John Knox Press, 1994), are overly confident in their efforts to find a key to Jesus' teaching in his cultural context and perspective. Similarly, efforts to make a sharp distinction between the teaching of Jesus and that of the evangelists on the issue of possessions fail to impress; see, e.g., D. L. Mealand, *Poverty and Expectation in the Gospels* (London: SPCK, 1980); J. Nissen, *Poverty and Mission: New Testament Perspectives* (Leiden: Interuniversitair Instituut voor Missiologie en Oecumenica, 1984); L. Schottroff and W. Stegemann, *Jesus and the Hope of the Poor,* trans. M. J. O'Connell (Maryknoll, NY: Orbis Books, 1986). Of quite a different character, even though it appeals to a faulty reconstruction of first-century conditions, is the moving book by Howard Thurman, *Jesus and the Disinherited* (New York: Abingdon-Cokesbury Press, 1949).

studies that examine the dynamics of a specific writing, such as Luke-Acts or James, in light of reconstructed social realities, but even here, the actual exegetical yield does not seem to correspond to the effort expended.[13] Most useful is the sort of study that illuminates a range of passages because it locates a fundamental social dynamic.[14] Even at their best, however, such studies do not offer more than a sharper sense of the historical context of the New Testament's language. They do not directly, or even indirectly, help in the task of thinking theologically about possessions in the life of faith today.

Three studies provide both a close look at the specific Lukan themes and passages concerning possessions, and do so with an eye toward the question of their normative import. By far the most thorough work is, unfortunately for American readers, in German; but it is a splendid analysis of the Lukan witness.[15] Although slender, perfectly straightforward and serviceable is John Gillman's *Possessions and the Life of Faith: A Reading of Luke-Acts.*[16] Walter Pilgrim's *Good News to the Poor: Wealth and Poverty in Luke-Acts,* which was actually published the same year as my own book — and often reviewed in tandem with it — offers a solid reading of the biblical evidence, especially in Luke-Acts. Although each offers good insight into the biblical text, none of these grapples with the issue of normativity.

Other publications provide insight into the way in which the scriptural witness was translated in the early church. A historical survey of patristic thought on the subject is provided by J. L. Gonzales, *Faith and Wealth: A History of Early Christian Ideas on the Origin, Significance, and Use of Money.*[17] A deeper engagement with specific figures and issues is found in the essays edited by S. R. Holman, *Wealth and Poverty in Early Church and Society.*[18] Carolyn Osiek, in turn, carries out a close, contex-

---

13. See, e.g., P. U. Maynard-Reid, *Poverty and Wealth in James* (Maryknoll, NY: Orbis Books, 1984); H. Moxnes, *The Economy of the Kingdom: Social Conflict and Economic Relations in Luke's Gospel* (Philadelphia: Fortress Press, 1988); J. H. Neyrey, *The Social World of Luke-Acts: Models for Interpretation* (Peabody, MA: Hendrickson, 1991).

14. See, e.g., L. W. Countryman, *The Rich Christian in the Church of the Early Empire: Contradictions and Accommodations* (Lewiston, NY: E. Mellen Press, 1980).

15. F. W. Horn, *Glaube und Handeln in der Theologie des Lukas* (Göttingen: Vandenhoeck & Ruprecht, 1983).

16. Zacchaeus Studies New Testament (Collegeville, MN: Liturgical Press, 1991).

17. San Francisco: Harper and Row, 1990; see also B. Gordon, *The Economic Problem in Biblical and Patristic Thought* (Leiden: Brill, 1989).

18. Holy Cross Studies in Patristic Theology and History (Grand Rapids: Baker Academic Books, 2008).

tual reading of a single composition in *Rich and Poor in the* Shepherd of Hermas: *An Exegetical-Social Investigation.*[19] Such studies, like those devoted to historical context and New Testament themes, represent solid scholarship, but do not pose or respond to the theological or existential question concerning the Christian use of possessions today.

The opposite is the case for another set of publications that directly address the church as church. All of them are confident concerning the clarity of the biblical text, and challenge the church not only to identify with the poor, but also to attack the social, political, and economic structures that perpetuate poverty. The simplest of these are heartfelt calls to heed the words of the prophets and Jesus.[20] Others adopt a consistent liberationist model and attack what is regarded as the essentially destructive tendencies of capitalism.[21] Noteworthy in this group are the books written and edited by Leonardo Boff.[22] An early twenty-first-century report by the World Council of Churches, based on a survey of members throughout the world, suggests that the liberation model has not gained unchallenged ascendancy even in economically disadvantaged areas.[23] A more nuanced and impressive study in this category is R. J. Sider's *Rich Christians in an Age of Hunger,* which begins with concrete facts concerning the rich and poor in the world, recognizes the diversity of the biblical witness, and provides specific models for Christian action.[24]

For the most part, the historical and exegetical studies tend to ne-

---

19. The Catholic Biblical Quarterly Monograph Series 15 (Washington: Catholic Biblical Association of America, 1983).

20. See, e.g., C. Boerma, *The Rich, the Poor — and the Bible* (Philadelphia: Westminster, 1978), and E. Gatti, *Rich Church — Poor Church? Some Biblical Perspectives* (Maryknoll, NY: Orbis Books, 1974).

21. See especially H. Gollwitzer, *The Rich Christians and Poor Lazarus,* trans. D. Cairns (Edinburgh: Saint Andrew Press, 1970).

22. See L. Boff, *When Theology Listens to the Poor,* trans. R. R. Baur (San Francisco: Harper & Row, 1988); *Cry of the Earth, Cry of the Poor* (Maryknoll, NY: Orbis Books, 1997); *The People of God Amidst the Poor,* ed. L. Boff and V. Elizondo, trans. M. Lefebre (Edinburgh: T. & T. Clark, 1984); *Ecology and Poverty: Cry of the Earth, Cry of the Poor,* ed. L. Boff and V. Elizondo (London: SCM Press, 1995); *Option for the Poor: Challenge to the Rich Countries,* ed. L. Boff and V. Elizondo (Edinburgh: T. & T. Clark, 1986).

23. M. Taylor, *Christianity, Poverty and Wealth: The Findings of "Project 21"* (London: SPCK, 2003).

24. R. J. Sider, *Rich Christians in an Age of Hunger,* revised and expanded edition (Downers Grove, IL: InterVarsity Press, 1984).

glect the dimension of appropriation and action. For the most part, the studies addressing the response of the church are abstract in three ways: (a) they speak of "the church" in terms of national or international organization more than in terms of local assembly; (b) they simplify the biblical witness by reducing it to one strand; (c) they by-pass the question of human dispositions of faith and idolatry altogether and focus exclusively on structural social change. An exception to these tendencies is *The Word on the Street: Performing the Scriptures in the Urban Context,* by Stanley Saunders and Charles Campbell.[25] Arising from the authors' very specific work among the homeless of Atlanta, this series of essays and sermons reveals a passionate embrace both of the scriptural witness and of the particular and complex ways of being poor in a wealthy American city.

Corresponding to the oversimplification of the biblical witness in some books written for the church is a simplistic notion of economics generally. As I have tried to argue, the biblical basis for a strict community of possessions is slender and suspect. A community of possessions larger than a small intentional community (such as a monastery) can lead to both a loss of liberty and a lack of wealth. Three books help complicate the economic issue. Donald H. Nash, *Poverty and Wealth: The Christian Debate over Capitalism,* is especially valuable as an economic primer.[26] A vigorous debate over an economics compatible with Christian ideals is found in the essays edited by R. G. Clouse, *Wealth and Poverty: Four Christian Views of Economics.*[27] More bracing and challenging still is the classic defense of "spiritual capitalism" by G. F. Gilder in *Wealth and Poverty.*[28]

Several books have appeared in recent years that help negotiate the difficult passage from biblical text to ethical action in the world. Two are of broad general usefulness even though they do not make possessions a central topic: B. C. Birch and L. L. Rasmussen, *Bible and Ethics in the Christian Life,*[29] and R. B. Hays, *The Moral Vision of the New Testament: A Contemporary Introduction to New Testament Ethics.*[30] Two further books

25. Grand Rapids: Eerdmans, 2000.

26. Westchester, IL: Crossway Books, 1986.

27. Downers Grove, IL: InterVarsity Press, 1984.

28. New York: Basic Books, 1981.

29. Minneapolis: Augsburg, 1989. The saying of Jesus, "you always have the poor with you," is discussed on pp. 176-79.

30. San Francisco: HarperSanFrancisco, 1996. Hays turns to the sharing of possessions in his conclusion, pp. 462-70.

give substantial attention to the problem of moving from biblical prescription to Christian action with respect to possessions. S. E. Wheeler,
Wealth as Peril and Obligation: The New Testament on Possessions, is a
methodologically self-aware consideration of specific passages, in each
case moving from a close reading of the passage to a consideration of its
"moral use."[31] Even more elaborately, A. Verhey's *Remembering Jesus:
Christian Community, Scripture, and the Moral Life* examines the scriptural witness within "the world of Adam Smith," proposing that the
church continue its tradition of "justice and generosity."[32] Finally, there
are thoughtful essays in the collection edited by W. Schweiker and
C. Mathewes, *Having: Property and Possession in Religious and Social
Life.*[33]

Despite the quantity and quality of books produced since the first
edition of *Sharing Possessions* in 1981, it is safe to say that none of them
displays the same combination of elements, especially the serious commitment to thinking about possessions within the theological drama of
faith and idolatry. Perhaps this is because readers found the elements in
the manner I brought them together objectionable. Some certainly did.

Response to Critics

Reviewers of the first edition were not unkind; some, indeed, praised my
effort, suggesting that no one had put the question this way before,[34]
that my analysis was "masterful,"[35] that my study was "provocative"[36]
and "challenging," and a "breath of fresh air."[37] All the early reviews

31. Grand Rapids: Eerdmans, 1995.

32. Grand Rapids: Eerdmans, 2002. Verhey's discussion of economics extends from
p. 243 to p. 332.

33. Grand Rapids: Eerdmans, 2004. As in all scholarly collections, there are both
strong and weak essays, but noteworthy are those by P. D. Miller, "Property and Possessions in Light of the Ten Commandments" (pp. 17-50); M. M. Mitchell, "Silver Chamber
Pots and Other Goods Which Are Not Good: John Chrysostom's Discourse against Wealth
and Possessions" (pp. 88-121); W. Schweiker, "Reconsidering Greed" (pp. 249-71); and
D. McCloskey, "Avarice, Prudence, and the Bourgeois Virtues" (pp. 312-36).

34. J. Kodell, *Benedictines* 37 (1982-83): 38-42.

35. D. George, *Review and Expositor* 81 (1984): 338-39.

36. D. Goldsmith, *Saint Luke's Journal of Theology* 27 (1983): 72-74.

37. L. A. Taylor, *Christian Century* 99 (1982): 516; E. Hensell, *Catholic Biblical Quarterly*
45 (1983): 490.

agreed that approaching the issue of possessions from the perspective of the theological drama of faith and idolatry had value. Despite such positive notices, the reviewers also raised critical questions. Four such questions in particular, I think, deserve some response. The first two focus on my critical observations on the community of possessions and almsgiving; the third objects to my lack of clear moral guidance, and the fourth complains about the attention I gave to the discussion of human being and having.[38]

1. The most consistent objection to my analysis was my criticism of a community of possessions and my preference for almsgiving as an expression of sharing that was most compatible with the obedience of faith. As a former Benedictine monk, I was not at all surprised to find one monastic reviewer state that my "polemic against the community of goods is a bit overdone," that almsgiving also has had its abuses, and that "Scripture does not directly make almsgiving the normative expression of sharing for Christians."[39] Similarly, in a review essay that was extraordinarily open and generous toward the study as a whole, another monastic reviewer considered my analysis to provide the opportunity for monastic self-reflection, while rejecting the notion that everything in my analysis was accurate with respect to actual monastic practice.[40]

At the time of writing, however, I was not yet aware of how widely Christians had embraced a socialist vision, particularly in Europe as a result of the Christian-Marxist dialogue in East Germany. Nor was I yet aware of how the subsequent development in Latin America of Liberation Theology (on the same premises) had made the "community of possessions" option appear as scripturally and morally obvious to many — as was God's "preferential option for the poor." Nor had I yet grasped completely how my emphasis on moral/religious dispositions (faith and idolatry) went against the grain of the conviction shared by these same Christians that the change of societal structures was of greater urgency than the transformation of the human heart — or, perhaps better stated, the change of societal structures was the condition for the transformation of the human heart.

Thus, I was slow to decode the negative comments of some reviewers.

---

38. Alas, I have no adequate response to the complaint that the book was tedious and my writing careless (R. B. Savid in *Commonweal*).

39. E. Hensell, *Catholic Biblical Quarterly* 45 (1983): 491-92.

40. J. Kodell, *Benedictines* 37 (1982-83): 38-42.

It took some time and further reading to grasp the dismissive comment of the British reviewer, J. L. Houlden, that my defense of almsgiving was "a rather American preference" (understanding that "American" = "Capitalist," as "European" = "Socialist"), and as a conclusion to the whole discussion "rather a whimper than a bang" (that is, failing to address economic systems as such is a deficiency).[41] Another reviewer found that by "attacking most broad, communal attempts to establish equity and relinquish possessions as 'ideology,' Johnson glosses over Jesus' own strong words about the dangers of wealth and the biblical evidence of God's abiding desire for justice."[42] Only slow rereading helped me understand the reviewer's unstated premise that (God's) justice among humans is to be identified with a single form of communal expression.[43]

My response is to assert that my statements in the first edition are basically correct. A community of goods has proven to work best when it is practiced by a small intentional community — as in the case of monasticism. The more the practice finds expression at the level of a state economy, the greater grow the inherent dangers of social control, with the concomitant growth in the power of the controllers. Socialism as a society-wide economic system has today lost a considerable amount of its luster, because of a growing awareness of what ordinary people suffered under Soviet and Chinese Communist regimes. We have learned, as my analysis suggests, that the human heart by no means loses its idolatrous impulses toward avarice and greed simply because material possessions are removed from private control — those impulses continue to find expression in other realms, and even within the economic area. We have learned as well that while a community of possessions may do well at sharing wealth, it performs dismally as a producer of wealth.

More important, when I spoke of the tradition of almsgiving, I did not refer to the sort of "acts of random kindness" that ignore the deep dimensions of human need, or the "acts of beneficence" by wealthy patrons that give back in the form of monuments what might have been taken from others by means of unjust practices. Such seems to have been the way I was read by Allen Verhey, who states, "One may wonder whether Johnson's admirable contribution to the moral discernment of the Chris-

---

41. *Expository Times* 93 (1982): 249.

42. Robert Massie, Jr., in *Sojourners* 12 (1983): 42-43.

43. The same premises seem to underlie the mild critical statements made by J. Grassi, *Horizons* 10 (1983): 144-45.

tian community is sufficiently critical of the ways in which almsgiving, *or individual acts of charity,* can be (and has been) co-opted by an 'ideological' legitimation of laissez-faire capitalism" (emphasis added).[44]

By no means am I unaware of or uncritical of aspects of capitalism, especially as currently practiced. I do not affirm savage competition as the ideal model of human interaction. I do not approve of the commodification of identity and worth. I do not think that the natural resources of the planet should heedlessly be destroyed in order to serve luxury. Indeed, I take it as axiomatic that the biblical witness I adduced in the first edition condemns as unrighteous the moving of landmarks, the swallowing of the houses of widows, the use of unbalanced measures, the neglect of the endemically dispossessed in the land. I agree with James that "true religion" before God is measured by "visiting orphans and widows."

But I do not agree with those critics of capitalism who make it the cause of all poverty, and propose instead an economic system that promises to remove all poverty. People are widows and orphans because spouses and parents die; they are poor because of the vagaries of climate and topography, because of volcano and flood, because of poor choices and little talent, because of social collapse, war and revolution, because of injury and disease, because of psychological and cognitive incapacity, because of a lack of freedom and education. Economic systems — yes, forms of capitalism — can exacerbate such forms of poverty, but they do not of and by themselves exclusively create poverty. Nor can a structural change in an economy eliminate all these other causes of poverty. To think so is not to live in the real world.

Moreover, Verhey (and others) seem to have misread me — or perhaps I was dangerously obscure in my writing — when they think I was speaking about "individual acts of charity" when I write about the Jewish practice of almsgiving. Verhey continues from his previous sentence, "And one may wonder whether he is sufficiently attentive to the theological roots of communal responsibilities for meeting the needs of the poor." But it is precisely as a communal practice that I described Jewish almsgiving. I went into considerable detail, describing the appointment of collectors and distributors, the oversight of the board of elders, the careful discrimination between the distribution of daily food (the plate) and the long-term care for the dispossessed (the chest).

It is precisely as a communally organized form of response to the

44. A. Verhey, *Remembering Jesus,* p. 286.

needs of the poor that I recommended Christian consideration of the Jewish practice. This is not a matter of spontaneous and individualistic volunteerism; it is a matter of a consistent, organized, and communal effort over a period literally of thousands of years. We might remember that for Jews, the sharing of possessions in such fashion *is* a question of "justice" *(sedeqah),* a justice that is accomplished locally, communally, and responsively to the real needs of the community.

2. Some reviewers objected to my use of synagogal organized charity as a model for Christians. One complained because the Jewish texts were strange: "the extended reference to Jewish materials in the last chapter is a closed book to all but the initiated."[45] Another objected to the fact that "Johnson turns to Rabbinic sources rather than outlining a Christian rationale that takes into account Jesus' and Paul's teachings about the kingdom of God, judgment, grace, and redemption."[46] I confess to finding the first complaint puzzling. If this tradition flourishes and has been a witness to using possessions righteously, why should not Christians learn from it? A sharp response might be, "Shame on Christians for not knowing such texts!" A softer one might be, "These texts and traditions are an expression of faith from which Christians can — as in other matters — learn with profit."[47]

The second form of the objection is more troubling, for it (inadvertently, I am sure) expresses the all-too-common assumption that what is properly Christian is what is uniquely or distinctively Christian, as well as the assumption that proper "theology" must be based in the specific sayings of Jesus and the statements of Paul. The statement reveals a trace of the crypto-Marcionism that runs through too much Christian theology. More shocking, by treating these Jewish traditions as something alien, the criticism reveals ignorance of the fact that the community of possessions is not, in fact, based in Scripture, but in Greek Utopian thinking, whereas the sharing of possessions through almsgiving is profoundly and explicitly grounded in Torah.

Apart from Luke's depiction of the Jerusalem church in Acts 2:41-47 and 4:32-37, furthermore, the actual *practices* of sharing possessions

---

45. D. Goldsmith, *The Saint Luke's Journal of Theology* 27 (1983): 74.

46. R. Massie, *Sojourners* 12 (1983): 43.

47. Compare my argument concerning the lessons Christian hermeneutics can learn from Judaism, in L. T. Johnson, *The Writings of the New Testament: An Interpretation,* 2nd enlarged edition (Minneapolis: Fortress Press, 1999), pp. 612-13, and "Christians and Jews: Starting Over," *Commonweal* 130, no. 2 (2003): 15-19.

(koinonia) in the New Testament resemble Jewish practice more than they do a strict community of possessions. The feeding of widows in Acts 6:1-7 and Paul's discussion of the support of widows in 1 Timothy 5:3-16 clearly suppose the sort of community almsgiving such as was practiced in every Jewish community. Similarly, the support offered by the Philippians for Paul's work among Gentiles, and the support Paul sought from the Romans for his work in Spain do not suggest a structural community of possessions so much as the communal gathering and dispersal of funds for specific needs and goals. Likewise, the collection that Paul and his associates gathered from among Gentile churches for the saints in Jerusalem deploys the sort of delegates and volunteer offerings found in the Jewish materials. Far from being alien to Scripture, there is far more biblical support — in both testaments — for almsgiving of every kind than there is for a community of possessions.

3. One reviewer made a comment in passing that I want to seize on, in order to emphasize a point. Her comment? "Going into much detail (perhaps too much), Johnson examines the problem of 'human possessing' — the ownership of a Christian's own body — 'being' and 'having'."[48] Perhaps the reviewer meant nothing more by her "perhaps too much [detail]" than the *Commonweal* reviewer meant when he complained about my loose sentence structure. But if she meant that my opening inquiry into the language we use about having and my phenomenological reflections about the body were excessive, then she has touched on an important point, and one I want to contest.

Over the thirty years since I wrote this book, I have had the growing conviction that the single greatest deficiency in the theological and moral engagement with Scripture among Christians is the failure to exercise sufficient care in engaging "what is" in present human experience. We contest the biblical words concerning sexuality, for example, without adequately appreciating the mysterious and elusive reality of the human experience of sexuality (that very recent word). It is this feature of Allen Verhey's *Remembering Jesus* that I appreciate: he takes the time to actually look at the human phenomenon and get some handle on the shape of the question before asking what Scripture might have to say about it. The same quality is found in Margaret Farley's recent work; she insists that specific knowledge of the natural and social sciences with respect to sexuality is of fundamental importance for the responsible reading of the

48. D. George, *Review and Expositor* 81 (1984): 339.

scriptural witness.[49] I agree completely. Indeed, in all matters touching the body — and there are few significant issues that do not — theology needs to take much more seriously the need to begin with a patient and precise assessment of what the body reveals and conceals of the human spirit. Not only the individual but also the social body needs this sort of attention. The reading of Scripture can only be improved by such contemplation.

4. Two reviewers touched on my failure to provide concrete guidance for the faithful use of possessions. One concluded, "It's hard to fault Johnson's program, except that it depends overmuch on how folks *think* about themselves and their possessions. He still leaves largely dangling the answer to, 'What shall I do with all this stuff I've accumulated?'"[50] Another also concludes his review, "And it all leaves one hazy by what logic the Bible is now used, now refused, as a source for guidance for the present day."[51] Although these objections move in slightly different directions, they share the perception that I did not provide a clear answer to a problem. My effort to show that being and having properly are understood not in terms of problem but in terms of mystery — for which there can never be a simple and once-for-all "answer" — seems to have persuaded neither reviewer. But I stand by that distinction and its implications. How we think about ourselves and our projects of owning in the sight of God is always a key to the way in which we enact our faith and make use of our possessions (spiritual as well as material). Discernment, as I will try to show below, is a constant necessity even as it is a perilous enterprise. And because our selves and our projects remain resistant to easy reduction, so does the scriptural witness remain unstable and shifting. Not in its main emphasis, which is perfectly clear: possessions deriving from envy, covetousness, theft, oppression, and injustice are illegitimate; every form of possession must be shared with others. But the way in which faith variously discerns the faithful disposition of possessions requires discrimination among the biblical witnesses. Sharing possessions as a symbol of faith demands the asceticism of attentiveness, just as the obedience that is faith demands a constant response to the concrete and changing circumstances of our lives.

49. M. Farley, *Just Love: A Framework for Christian Sexual Ethics* (New York: Continuum International, 2006).

50. M. I. Wegener, *Currents in Theology and Mission* 10 (1983): 111.

51. J. L. Houlden, *The Expository Times* 93 (1982): 249.

Afterthoughts

As I continued to think, teach, and write about possessions over the thirty years since this book first appeared, I grew in appreciation of certain aspects of the topic that I did not consider or did not sufficiently develop. This new edition provides the opportunity to touch on them and at least point readers to fuller and better treatments.

1. Hospitality

The welcoming of others into one's own space is a common practice and virtue in earliest Christianity. Luke-Acts is once more a valuable witness to the practice. Luke uses the reception of Jesus by Martha and Mary and the rejection of him by Pharisees at banquets as narrative examples to express the acceptance and rejection of God's prophet and his message.[52] Jesus' sending of the twelve and the seventy to extend his proclamation of God's rule and its enactment through healing depends on the hospitality of others.[53] As the apostles move from Jerusalem to Rome and from Jew to Gentile with the good news, the acceptance and rejection of God's emissaries amounts to the acceptance or rejection of their message.[54]

The New Testament epistolary literature attests to the importance of the social practice of hospitality by churches. The second and third letters of John provide a window into an early conflict between leaders of household churches and the way in which hospitality was both valued as a way of supporting wandering missionaries and was used as an instrument in the clash between different understandings of the good news.[55]

---

52. By juxtaposing the hostile question of the lawyer concerning "the neighbor" — to which Jesus answers with the parable of the Samaritan (Luke 10:25-37) — and the story of Martha and Mary (Luke 10:38-42), Luke places the theme of human hospitality within the framework of the acceptance and rejection of God's prophet; see the discussion in L. T. Johnson, *The Gospel of Luke*, Sacra Pagina 3 (Collegeville, MN: Liturgical Press, 1991), pp. 171-76.

53. For discussion of the two sendings within the literary context of Luke's Journey Narrative, see Johnson, *The Gospel of Luke*, pp. 144-71.

54. See Acts 9:32-43; 10:23-24; 16:11-15; 17:11-13; 18:3-4; 18:26-27; 20:1-3; 21:8-14; 28:1-10.

55. See the splendid study by A. J. Malherbe, "Hospitality and Inhospitality in the Church," in *Social Aspects of Early Christianity*, 2nd ed. (Philadelphia: Fortress Press, 1983); also, J. Koenig, *New Testament Hospitality: Partnership with Strangers as Promise and Mission* (Eugene, OR: Wipf & Stock, 2001).

Paul's letters reveal how he depended on and encouraged hospitality both for himself and his colleagues as a condition for his far-reaching mission.[56]

For Paul, however, hospitality was also a moral disposition exercised within the community. Even as he seeks to persuade the Roman church to welcome his emissary Phoebe and provide whatever she needed to organize support for Paul's mission to Spain (Rom. 15:14–16:2), he exhorts them to accept each other despite their differences: "Welcome (or receive) one another, then, as Christ has welcomed (or received) you, for the glory of God" (Rom. 15:7).[57] The letter to the Hebrews similarly tells readers, "Let mutual love continue. Do not neglect hospitality, for through it some have unknowingly entertained angels" (Heb. 13:1-2).[58]

My discussion of sharing possessions in the body of this book emphasizes the giving of what one has to others, material things, yes, but also everything over which we might claim ownership: time, ideas, relationships, values, even virtues. The emphasis was on the movement outward. As the fine studies devoted to the theological dimensions of hospitality have shown, the movement here is the opposite: not in actions of giving but in gestures of receiving.[59] At the physical level, hospitality makes space for another. But that mode of reception symbolizes an openness and receptivity of the other along the same spectrum as other forms of sharing possessions: welcoming the presence of the other, sharing time, receiving new ideas, welcoming the new even when it threatens the accustomed. When the other is received as other, then hospitality is

56. For Paul, see Rom. 15:30–16:3; 1 Cor. 16:1-9; 2 Cor. 6:11-13; 7:2-4; 13:1-10; Gal. 4:4; 1 Thess. 2:13; for his delegates, see 1 Cor. 4:17; 16:11; Eph. 6:21-22; Phil. 2:19-30; Col. 4:7-10; 1 Thess. 3:1-6; Titus 3:12; Philem. 12-17.

57. For the basically fundraising purpose of Romans, see L. T. Johnson, *Reading Romans: A Literary and Theological Commentary* (Macon, GA: Smyth & Helwys, 2001), pp. 1-18, and for mutual hospitality as the expression of righteousness in the community, see pp. 209-21.

58. For discussion, see L. T. Johnson, *Hebrews: A Commentary,* The New Testament Library (Louisville: Westminster John Knox, 2006), pp. 336-42.

59. See, e.g., H. J. M. Nouwen, *Reaching Out: The Three Movements of the Spiritual Life* (Garden City, NY: Doubleday, 1975); B. Byrne, *The Hospitality of God: A Reading of Luke's Gospel* (Collegeville, MN: Liturgical Press, 2000); T. W. Ogletree, *Hospitality to the Stranger: Dimensions of Moral Understanding* (Philadelphia: Fortress Press, 1985); T. R. Hawkins, *Sharing the Search: A Theology of Christian Hospitality* (Nashville: The Upper Room, 1987); D. C. Bass, ed., *Practicing Our Faith: A Way of Life for a Searching People* (San Francisco: Jossey-Bass, 1997).

truly an expression of the obedience of faith. Paradoxically, when space is truly made for the other in our lives, the most important consequence is not that the guest receives a gift from us, but that we are gifted by those who enter our lives.

Especially in light of my critical comments on the community of possessions, I am delighted to recognize that this is a form of sharing possessions particularly suited to such a way of life, as demonstrated by the prominent role played by hospitality in all forms of Christian monasticism. The classic expression of this ideal, indeed, is found in the *Rule of Benedict*, which gives particular attention to the ways guests are to be welcomed: "All guests that come should be received as would be the person of Christ . . . let the greeting of the guest, both at their arrival and upon their departure, be done with every mark of humility, with bowed head or with one's whole body prostrate upon the ground, thus honoring in him the person of Christ, who is really being so welcomed." And again, with the Christian idealism and realistic insight into humans typical of Benedict, "Let most conscientious care be shown to the poor and to strangers, for in them Christ is truly welcome; for the powerful impression which wealth and high station inspire creates its own peculiar esteem."[60]

The disposition to hospitality is an expression of the obedience of faith. By making room for the other and inviting the other to share in her life, the hospitable person relativizes her own project, allows her own "sense of place" to be less than absolute, refuses to cling to her own things as untouchable by others. One of the theologically attractive aspects of hospitality is its elasticity: it can stretch from the level of the individual professor willing to learn new ideas, to the family able to welcome a stranger, to the neighborhood open to new residents, to a city receptive to different customs, to a nation willing to receive immigrants.

2. Stewardship

I only became aware of the pertinence of my thought to the dimension of ecclesial life called stewardship when I was invited, after the book's publication, to address several stewardship conferences. Those who invited me were, I confess, more hospitable to my thoughts than I initially was to

60. *Rule of Benedict,* chap. 53.

their concerns. The image of hospitality is apt, for to a Roman Catholic the term "stewardship" carried a distinctly Protestant, that is, alien guise, so that my first response was one of suspicion. Wasn't this just a fancy term used to manipulate people into providing financial support for the institutional church? This suspicion grew greater as I began to survey some of the literature devoted to the subject.[61] I remain reluctant to follow some stewardship enthusiasts in making sweeping claims for the image.[62] I have nevertheless come to a greater appreciation of this biblical term.

The image arises from the social setting of earliest Christianity, which located itself in the household *(oikos)*. The role of the steward or household manager *(oikonomos)* was a common feature especially in the "great houses" with a more elaborate structure: the manager — sometimes himself a slave — was below the owner or "Master of the household" *(oikodespotes,* Luke 14:21), and over the other "household servants" *(oiketai)* through whom the work of the household was accomplished. Since the time of Socrates' student Xenophon, serious philosophical thought was given to the proper ordering of the household *(oikonomia).*[63] It was natural for Paul, establishing churches in such households, to apply the imagery of stewardship to his ministry. Thus he speaks of himself and Apollos as "servants of God and stewards of the mysteries of God." He continues, "Now of course it is required of stewards that they be found trustworthy" (1 Cor. 4:1-2). The steward's responsibility, therefore, has at least three dimensions: he must please the master, work for the benefit of other servants, and do both by showing a responsible use of the resources entrusted to his care.

This quality of trustworthiness *(pistos)* is thematic in two of Jesus' parables found in Luke's Gospel. In 12:41-48, Jesus speaks of "the faithful and prudent manager" *(oikonomos)* as one who serves the master by pro-

---

61. The "Library of Christian Stewardship" contains such titles as *Christian Stewardship and Ecumenical Confrontation* (by T. K. Thompson, 1961), *Stewardship in Mission* (by W. T. Thomas, 1964), and *The Christian Meaning of Money* (by O. A. Piper, 1965), next to *Handbook of Stewardship Procedures* (by T. K. Thompson, 1964), *Stewardship Illustrations* (by T. K. Thompson, 1965), and *Why People Give* (by M. E. Carlson, 1968).

62. See, e.g., D. J. Hall, *The Steward: A Biblical Symbol Come of Age,* Library of Christian Stewardship (New York: Friendship Press, 1982), and especially, J. Reumann, *Stewardship and the Economy of God,* Library of Christian Stewardship (Grand Rapids: Eerdmans, 1992).

63. Xenophon, *Oecumenicus.*

viding allowance of food to others at the proper time, in contrast to the wicked slave (also serving as household manager), who "begins to beat the other slaves, men and women, and to eat and drink and get drunk." In 16:1-9, Jesus tells the story of the dishonest steward *(oikonomos)* who cheated his master by squandering his property; when faced with dismissal, he cancels the debts of others so that they will "welcome him" after he is fired. Jesus wants his hearers to understand the story as an analogy: the steward was "clever" *(phronimos)* even as he was unfaithful; they are to be equally "discerning" *(phronimos)* in their faithful use of possessions (Luke 16:10-13).

The image of the steward is valuable when thinking about possessions for two reasons: first, it is essentially communal and relational — the steward is defined by a relationship to the one under whom he serves and the ones whom he serves; second, the element of "trustworthiness" or responsibility is a way of rendering "the obedience of faith": the appropriate way of taking care of another's possessions and using them for the welfare of others is not entirely predictable, and requires prudence or cleverness or discernment *(phronimos)*. It is an image that works especially well in thinking about the human vocation with respect to the earth. A proper sense of stewardship engenders dispositions and actions that preserve and nurture God's creation, rather than distort and destroy it.[64]

The ideal of stewardship is, however, itself distorted when it is reduced to a means of eliciting financial and other support for the institutional church. Unfortunately, this is the arena in which such language is most frequently found. There is every reason for Christians to support the institutional church with their resources; it is an aspect of good citizenship within the community of faith. But such support need not have a theological legitimation, and the willingness to use the New Testament's language as a form of fundraising motivation seems at least slightly disordered. Far better for churches to think of stewardship, not in terms of how they raise money for the upkeep or maintenance of their plant and program, but in terms of how they might use the church's resources in service of God's rule. Such sharing of possessions is a matter of the dis-

---

64. This point is well made by D. J. Hall, in *Imaging God: Dominion as Stewardship*, Library of Christian Stewardship (New York: Friendship Press, 1986), and *The Stewardship of Life in the Kingdom of Death*, Library of Christian Stewardship (Grand Rapids: Eerdmans, 1988).

cernment of faith, and ought to be responsive to the real needs of those within and outside the community. A community form of almsgiving would be one expression of such stewardship, but it also does not exhaust the possibilities of God's call to move from idolatry to the obedience of faith.

3. *Sabbath*

Sabbath observance is another Jewish practice from which Christians can learn much.[65] I have begun to use this as an example when the question is put to me by congregations with whom I have been thinking about the faithful use of possessions, and they ask, "What can we do?" As a thought experiment, I propose that we seriously consider what it would mean for a local congregation to observe Sabbath — for Christians, to be sure, this would mean Sunday. I suggest Sabbath observance precisely as a means of making a communal prophetic statement concerning possessions.

As classically expressed in Torah, the Sabbath had a twofold dimension. Negatively, Jews were to refrain from the work activities of ordinary days in order to rest, as God had rested on the seventh day from the labors of creation. Positively, this day was dedicated to the worship of God and the study of Torah. The two dimensions fit perfectly the double aspect of the obedience of faith. Idolatry is essentially seeking life through "the works of our hands," to treat possessions of every sort as the source and sustainer of our being, identity, and blessing. Intentionally to cease from such labor, even for a short time, is to declare liberation from the compulsive clutches of idolatry. To dedicate a day totally to the worship and study of God, similarly, is to express the obedience of faith, declaring that in God's power only is truly to be found life and blessing.

Christians who do not share the millennia-long tradition of Jews face serious difficulties in beginning such a practice. The first is actually shaping a communal commitment; since Christianity has become so

---

65. See, e.g., D. C. Bass, *Practicing Our Faith: A Way of Life for a Searching People* (San Francisco: Jossey-Bass, 1997); M. J. Dawn, *The Sense of the Call: A Sabbath Way of Life for Those Who Serve God, the Church, and the World* (Grand Rapids: Eerdmans, 2006); K. Hirsch, *A Sabbath Life: A Woman's Search for Wholeness* (New York: North Point Press, 2001); W. Muller, *Sabbath: Finding Rest, Renewal, and Delight in Our Busy Lives* (New York: Bantam Books, 2000).

pervasively individualistic, forming a shared commitment to a practice is difficult both to conceive and execute. The second is determining the very thing that Jewish midrash spent so much effort deciding — how should this day represent a "rest" that distinguishes it from the other six days? The third is providing the positive communal content of the Sabbath observance — what would be the Christian equivalent to the study of Torah, for example?

Even as a thought experiment, the challenges are daunting. I have proposed to congregations, for example, that they begin by thinking small on the negative side. Suppose they pledge not to shop and buy on this one day? No sooner is the suggestion spoken than the difficulties it poses are evident. How can people working for stores that open on Sunday observe the rest? How can dual-career families with hectic schedules and no other times available take care of their family grocery and supply needs? It immediately becomes clear how deeply enmeshed all members of the congregation have become in the secular calendar that makes Sunday not just another shopping day, but the busiest day of buying and selling at the domestic level. It also quickly becomes clear that if such a practice were to be engaged by the community as such, support would need to be given to those members who do not have other times to shop; others in the community would need to help "bear their burdens" (Gal. 6:2) with respect to providing for their families, if such economically overdefined members are going to be able to share in the practice.

Thinking through the Sabbath observance on the positive side is equally challenging. Again, even starting small reveals the church's condition of enmeshment in the secular definition of reality. What can be asked of congregants before they revolt, or bolt? Even such a simple matter of scheduling worship at a Sunday "prime time" reveals the ways in which allegiance to other powers supersedes explicit devotion to the Lord. Pastors who are so bold as to schedule worship so as to interfere with NFL football games (live or televised) come to understand the limits of Sabbath commitment. To a lesser degree, perhaps, many other activities — from soccer practice for the children to marathons for this cause or that — encroach on the scheduling of worship.

Such down-to-earth considerations help a community realize how Sabbath-day "buying and selling" is only the most obvious manifestation of lives defined by the world's idolatrous impulses, how time and space are also things that we "have," and how the way we dispose of them reveals among us patterns of idolatry and faith. But however clumsily and with whatever difficulty, such efforts to establish a Sabbath observance also show how the Christian community's faithful use of possessions might stand as a prophetic witness of faith in the living God as a way of expressing "holiness," a way of being in the world that is other than the world's way, and witnessing to the sovereignty of God.

4. Discernment

My discussions of hospitality, stewardship, and Sabbath have shown how important discernment is in the obedience of faith. At the level of individual response, discernment is required for the faithful disposition of possessions. There are always more needs in the world than there are resources to meet those needs. Each person of faith must, therefore, exercise the virtue of prudence (another way of speaking of discernment) in specific circumstances. Faith requires of me that I share the gifts God has given, and continues to give me. But how I share those gifts, and which gifts I share in which circumstances, cannot be decided once for all. My most obvious gift may be speaking and writing as a teacher. But my wife and child do not need this from me nearly so much as they need my time and attention. Even my students may need, at this particular moment, something other than my rhetorical and literary skill. They may need a safe space, or the same sort of time and attention that my family needs.

Several years ago, the graduating class at the Candler School of Theology (where I have taught for seventeen years) asked me to sing solo at their final worship service. The request frightened me. I had not sung solo in public for over thirty years and was acutely aware of my musical limitations. But my students apparently did not need my words nearly so much as they needed my presence, and that in a manner that revealed my frail humanity. I agreed to do it, and I practiced, and on the appointed day, I sang the song (poorly). What others need from us, I knew, may not be the gifts we like best to give. The asceticism of attentiveness is required to discern the appropriate mode of sharing at every moment. Without such discernment of how God is calling us within the concrete circumstances of everyday life — concretely in the other with whom I now am — we are all too likely to share, not as an expression of the obedience of faith, but as an expression of our own idolatrous project of control (I choose how I want to give rather than the gift you need).[66]

Such discernment is both more necessary and more difficult in the case of the community's disposition of possessions. Even when we conceive of stewardship as the community's faithful use of possessions, it is not always clear — in fact it is seldom clear — how possessions should be shared in a specific situation. Should the church use its collection money for new hymnals or for an enlarged soup kitchen for indigent residents of the neighborhood? The answer is not as obvious as many in the community might suppose; indeed, it is likely that different segments of the community might find different options "obvious." Discussions of financial decisions in congregations can quickly become fractious for the same reasons they do in our families — the acquisition and disposition of possessions is fraught with diverse meanings for different people.

It is important for congregations to learn the practices of discernment in small matters so that they are not torn asunder by the need to make hard decisions in large matters. Members need to learn how making the "right" decision is often less important than making a decision "righteously." They must together learn to listen to the various ways in which God works within and outside the community, as preparation for the discernment of how their faith might be obedient with respect to possessions. When they gather together regularly in the name of Jesus to read Scripture, to share their faith-stories, and to seek wisdom in the living of their faith, such congregants already are practicing a form of hospitality in the way they welcome one another as Christ has welcomed them, and are already sharing with each other the most important possessions of time, space, energy, attention, and careful thought.[67]

---

66. See the discussion in L. T. Johnson, *Faith's Freedom: A Classic Spirituality for Contemporary Christians* (Minneapolis: Fortress Press, 1990), pp. 78-96, 99-113, and 174-85.

67. See L. T. Johnson, *Scripture and Discernment: Decision Making in the Church* (Nashville: Abingdon Press, 1996).

Study Questions

A book like *Sharing Possessions* that invites readers into a process of thinking about a subject of great importance to the life of faith can certainly be read and appreciated by individuals, but the best way to read it is probably within the context of a group of fellow Christians who are willing and able to risk sharing their own lives and thoughts with others. These questions are intended to stimulate the process of such sharing.

Introduction

The purpose of the introduction is to begin a process of thinking that starts with the readers themselves. The more the process begins here, the richer the subsequent reading.

1. What do we mean when we use certain words involving possessions? What do I claim when I say I have "earned" something? That I "own" something? That something is "mine"? Think about the connotations of terms like "rich" and "poor." How are such terms relative (to each other)? How are "rich" and "poor" both qualitative and quantitative in their meaning? Which term do you apply to yourself? Why?

2. Think through — or talk through — the implications of terms like "being" and "having" when applied to the body. What happens if we consider the body only as something we "have"? What is the consequence if we deny that we do "have" bodies and can dispose of them? Why are being a body and having a body both important in being a person? How does this relate to wealth and poverty?

3. This is a book that spends a lot of time examining Scripture. Why do you think it important to include Scripture in thinking about possessions and the life of faith? What do you mean by "taking the Bible seriously"? In what sense is the biblical text normative for you, or for your faith community?

Chapter 1
Searching for a Mandate

1. Discuss the premise that the Bible presents clear norms for Christian behavior. Is this true in all cases? How does Luke-Acts complicate things with respect to possessions?
2. Why are the ideals of radical poverty and almsgiving in tension with each other?
3. Why does this chapter make no mention of "tithing"? Is there any text of the New Testament that does speak of tithing? Do you consider tithing a personal obligation? Why or why not?
4. Does the New Testament provide any support for the so-called "prosperity gospel"?
5. What sort of selectivity do you — or your denomination — practice when it comes to the ideal way of sharing possessions?

Chapter 2
Toward a Theological Understanding of Possessions

1. Discuss the premise that "understanding shapes actions." Is it true that how we think about things affects the way we use things? Why or why not?
2. Discuss some of the examples of body language provided by this chapter, especially the connection between body language and possessions. Do "open arms" and a "generous spirit" really go together?
3. Consider the ways body symbolism is culturally diverse. Think about controversies involving hair, costume, adornment, and gestures.
4. How is idolatry defined in this chapter? How does the logic of idolatry lead to the hoarding of possessions? If being is equated with having, can I share my possessions?
5. How does the logic of faith — defined as the openness to the mystery of God in trust and obedience — lead to the sharing of our possessions?

6. Discuss how the "faith of Jesus" as portrayed in the Gospels presents a model of "poverty" as a dimension of faithful obedience to God. How is Christ's poverty an example for our use of possessions?

7. Returning to your own life, think (or talk) about the way this chapter expands the notion of being and having in light of faith. Name some of the "things" we can claim as our own, or share.

Chapter 3
Sharing Possessions: Mandate and Symbol of Faith

1. Discuss the proposition that possessions are not good or bad in themselves, but in what they mean. How do they symbolize and affect our response to the specific circumstances of our lives?

2. Is there a genuine connection between the theological principle of righteousness through faith and the faithful use of possessions? What does the way you use possessions say about your life of faith?

3. Is it true that "how we view God determines our view of other people"? Why or why not?

4. Is it true that "how we respond to other people is how we respond to God"? Why or why not?

5. Why is the New Testament Letter of James such a valuable witness to the faithful use of possessions?

6. This chapter surveys the teaching on possessions in the Law, Prophets, Writings, Letter of James, and the Gospels. What do you see as the major points of continuity in all those biblical books? What are the main points of difference? How does this inform your own understanding of the use of possessions?

7. How does this chapter's section on "the ways of sharing" apply to the concrete circumstances of your life?

Chapter 4
Critical Observations on
the Community of Goods and Almsgiving

1. How does this discussion flow naturally from the final section of the previous chapter, called "Theology and Ideology"?

2. Discuss and evaluate the positive and negative aspects of having a community of goods in light of earlier chapters.

3. Distinguish between the practice of almsgiving by individuals and a community's organized practice of almsgiving.

4. Discuss the importance of discernment — for both individuals and communities — in making specific decisions concerning the way possessions are shared. Is the sharing of possessions something that needs to be an ongoing faith practice for you or your community?

Suggestions for Further Reading

The following list is highly selective. Some books or articles touch directly upon matters treated in this book, whether in agreement or not; others provide potentially helpful background material; and others have informed the author's mind in a less direct fashion.

Berger, P. *The Sacred Canopy.* Garden City, NY: Anchor Books, 1969. Representative of the works by Berger that have influenced the perspectives of the Introduction and chapter 2 of this book.

Brueggemann, W. *The Land.* Overtures to Biblical Theology. Philadelphia: Fortress Press, 1977, pp. 45-70, 90-106. A book from this series that deals tangentially with the matters of chapter 3.

Cohn, N. *The Pursuit of the Millennium.* New York: Harper Torchbooks, 1961. Traces the ideal of community sharing with apocalyptic movements, particularly Münster.

Dahl, N. A. "Paul and Possessions," in *Studies in Paul.* Minneapolis: Augsburg, 1977. A typically sane and solid treatment of Paul's attitude toward possessions.

Degenhardt, H.-J. *Lukas Evangelist der Armen.* Stuttgart: Verlag Katholisches Bibelwerk, 1965. A frequently cited work on Luke-Acts, wrong in many ways, but with good remarks in an appendix on possessions at Qumran.

Dupont, J. *Les Béatitudes.* 3 vols. Vol. 1. Louvain: Editions Nauwelaerts, 1958. Vols. 2 and 3. Paris: J. Gabalda, 1969, 1973. Magisterial work on the Beatitudes with exhaustive discussion of issues and incisive exegesis.

Gelin, A. *The Poor of Yahweh.* Translated by K. Sullivan. Collegeville, MN: Liturgical Press, 1964. A popular classic still worth reading on the development of "spiritual poverty" in the tradition.

Grant, R. M. *Early Christianity and Society.* New York: Harper & Row, 1977. A helpful historical survey of Christian social realities and attitudes.

Hands, A. R. *Charities and Social Aid in Greece and Rome.* London: Thames &

Hudson, 1968. Outlook and institutions concerning beneficence in the Greco-Roman world.

Hengel, M. *Property and Riches in the Early Church.* Philadelphia: Fortress Press, 1974. From the historical perspective, a brief but effective treatment of pre-Christian and Christian views on property and wealth. It concludes with pastorally pertinent theses.

Johnson, L. T. *The Literary Function of Possessions in Luke-Acts.* SBLDS 39. Missoula, MT: Scholars Press, 1977. Provides the exegetical backing for much of chapter 1 of this book.

Kantor, R. *Commitment and Community.* Cambridge, MA: Harvard University Press, 1972. An analysis of nineteenth-century American communes that provides insight into perdurance of commitment techniques.

Karris, R. *What Are They Saying About Luke and Acts?* New York: Ramsey; Toronto: Paulist Press, 1979. Good short summary of major theological themes along with the author's view of Luke as a theology of the faithful God.

Keck, L. "The Poor among the saints in the New Testament," and "The poor among the saints in Jewish Christianity." *Zeitschrift für Neutestamentliche Wissenschaft* 56 (1965): 105-29, and 57 (1966): 54-78. Careful dissection of historical realities pertaining to possessions in Jerusalem, at Qumran, and among Ebionites.

Marcel, G. *Creative Fidelity.* Translated by R. Rosthal. New York: Farrar, Straus & Giroux, 1964. Perhaps the most accessible of his works. It is not just what Marcel says about being and having that is important, but the way he thinks.

Miranda, J. P. *Marx and the Bible.* Translated by J. Eagleson. Maryknoll, NY: Orbis Books, 1974. A polemical, learned book that uses the same texts as this one but reaches opposite conclusions.

Moore, G. F. *Judaism in the First Centuries of the Christian Era.* 2 vols. Vol. 2. New York: Schocken Books, 1971, pp. 162-79. The place to go for a start at learning about Jewish almsgiving.

Zablocki, B. *The Joyful Community.* Baltimore: Penguin Books, 1976. A sociological analysis of the Bruderhof community, with particularly good insight into pressures of spiritual conformity associated with community possessions.

Scripture Index

LIBRARY, UNIVERSITY OF CHESTER